Happily Married With Kids
It's Not a Fairy Tale

Will Use This Book as Resource

"Don't wait until it's too late to save your relationship! Dr. Carol Lindquist is an expert in couples' therapy, and in this book she shares her wisdom with the masses. You will gain practical tools for navigating universal parenting stressors, and emerge a stronger, healthier, happier family for having read it.

"I look forward to using this book as a resource in my practice." – *Jessica Drew de Paz, Psy.D., Laguna Beach, California*

Wish I Had Read This Book Three Decades Ago

"I enjoyed reading *Happily Married With Kids*, and found it to be an insightful and useful guide to parenting. I only wish I had that information about three decades ago. The book is a must-have and should be required reading to accompany a marriage license as well as birth certificate.

"Kudos." – *Laurie Parker, Esq. MBA, Temecula, California*

Hundreds of Helpful Ideas

"The book is a compilation of hundreds of helpful ideas to improve both marriage and parenting effectiveness. Dr. Lindquist uses both research and her many years of clinical experience to apply these practical ideas to the difficulties that many couples face.

"This book is not only a couples' handbook, nor just a parenting handbook, but emphasizes the interpersonal dynamics occurring between married couples while they are parents. Dr. Lindquist deals with many issues that parents face that are not often found in these types of books, including exhaustion from having a newborn, temptations to have an affair, stressful vacations, and sexual difficulties. I recommend this book, especially to couples struggling with their marriage while simultaneously raising children." – *F. Scott Ashdown, Psy.D., Licensed Psychologist, Sarasota/Venice, Florida*

Reviews of Dr. Carol's First Book

Great Book
"**...as if you had been looking in on our marriage.** I love the ideas and the encouragement that you offer. I am sure you have saved countless marriages! Okay, well, I have never in my life written to an author, regardless of how much I liked his or her book. But in this case, I just had to let you know…" –*Lindsay D.*

Written with wit
"**… while giving the reader excellent tips** on how to keep your marriage healthy... The author provides realistic suggestions for you to follow! This book is applicable to all stages of motherhood, and I highly recommend both the wife and husband reading it..." – *"A wife of 10 years who is having her first baby"*

My New Marriage Bible...
"**...has a good sense of humor.** I found many insights and helpful tips in this book. I wish I had found it sooner... I marked many pages and will be keeping this nearby to revisit and try ideas from..." –*"Reader" from Boston*

Good Book, Good Ideas
"**.... I only wish I/we had found it sooner.** It is written in plain English and really hits the mark in terms of things we've been dealing with. … who knew we might just be in a pretty normal

phase... it's an easy, enjoyable read and it gives me hope!" –*S. L. Myrick, Portland, Oregon*

Amazon.com Review
"**Nora Ephron said** that 'having an infant is like tossing a hand grenade into a marriage.' ... perhaps simple is the best place to start for couples trying to function on four hours of sleep. .... a worthy reference for couples short on sleep and patience, but desperately in need of quick solutions to bring the fun and connection back to their marriage." –*Erica Jorgensen*

Practical and Easy to Read
"**As a psychologist** working both with couples and individuals ... So often I have found that parents of young children feel very isolated and overwhelmed ... practical and easy to read, even when you have had an exhausting day with the kids ... focuses on solutions, recovery, and repair." –*Ira B. Poll*

Widsom, Warmth and Wit
"**As a pediatric/family psychologist** seeing dozens of families per month ... Dr. Lindquist's wisdom, warmth, and wit help every reader see the essential link between a healthy marriage and a healthy family foundation. It is the absolute best book of its kind ..." –*Linda Lifur-Bennett, Ph.D.*

Happily Married With Kids

Happily Married With Kids
IT'S NOT A FAIRY TALE

**Carol Ummel Lindquist,
Ph.D.**

Happily Married With Kids: It's Not a Fairy Tale

Copyright © 2011 by Carol Ummel Lindquist, Ph.D.

All rights reserved.

Granny Apple Publishing, LLC

Second Edition

This book is an updated revision of *Happily Married With Kids, It's Not Just a Fairy Tale,* Copyright © 2004 by Carol Ummel Lindquist, Ph.D. and published in 2004 by The Berkley Publishing Group, a division of Penguin Group (USA) Inc.

Although the information herein is based on the author's extensive experience and knowledge, it is not intended to substitute for the services of qualified professionals.

A complete list of credits appears on page 237.

Cataloging-in-Publication Data

Lindquist, Carol Ummel.

Happily married with kids : it's not a fairy tale / by Carol Ummel Lindquist. –

Granny Apple Publishing LLC trade pbk. Ed.

Includes bibliographical references.

ISBN: 0-983-13053-1

EAN-13: 978-0-9831305-3-6

1. Family and Relationships / Marriage 2. Family and Relationships/Parenting

PRINTED IN THE UNITED STATES OF AMERICA

Contents

Author's Note

I still remember the mysterious way people said to us, "Boy, is your life going to change!" when we said we had a new baby. Some said it with awe, some with dread, some with laughter. After a few years had passed, and with the birth of our second son, I no longer found these comments quite so mysterious.

As my personal adventures in marriage and parenting were evolving, my work as a clinical psychologist was becoming more and more focused on couples' therapy. With this convergence of interests, I began to take an almost voyeuristic interest in other parents' lives, focusing specifically on really happy couples who were successfully juggling two or three kids, two jobs, and everything else in between. I wanted to delve into the mystery, the magic and the laughter these successful couples had achieved.

I remembered the time, before kids, when Neil and I used to be like that and lamented that we had allowed our relationship to reach a point when we weren't even always very nice to each other. When I began shyly commenting on their apparent happiness, most of the happy couples freely admitted that it hadn't always been like that! Many of them said they had had a crisis and gone to counseling or a marriage retreat or had made a conscious decision to commit to love in their marriage.

Over time, I began to notice that what other couples fought about were exactly the same things that had triggered my fights with Neil. What's more, the particular fights couples seemed to have when their kids were two, three or five were the same fights Neil and I had had when our kids were those same ages. For example, as each of our kids reached two and my husband and I would go out with them socially, there was the

"Who doesn't pay enough attention to the children and whose turn is it to talk to the other adults" fight. At three, it is the "you are too lenient and no I am not" fight. Then, when our youngest was four or five, another couple visited with their two-year-old and had the same, "whose turn is it" argument. And so it was with the couples I counseled.

I also began to notice common threads among my happily married friends who seemed to roll right through the universal problems. They resolved issues in similar ways. I also noticed people began to resolve their fights and crises when their kids hit certain ages. For example, by four, parents aren't arguing about who is watching Johnny when they are out as a family any more, though they may be arguing about who picks him up from preschool and who arranges for the babysitter when they both have a breakfast meeting.

At five, mothers began to feel their children's in-dependence. When the youngest child reached five-and-a-half or six, moms often reported that this was the best year of their marriage since the kids were born. I also found similarities in couples who didn't seem to make it or who drifted apart—some just seemed to blow apart.

Can you remember when you first met? When you thought you had the same values and could talk for hours; thought your partner's quirks were cute and agreed on just about everything? Do you recall the times when you were so sexually attracted to each other that you got warm just thinking about being together? And, yes, you were actually excited to see each other.

If these memories are still in your mind—no matter how far back—I want to assure you that you can become the happiest couple on the block again. Even if you don't remember times like that but can remember what you really liked about your partner in the beginning, there is still a very good chance you can become a solidly happy and supportive team again. In fact, you can become closer and happier than you ever were.

In my practice I mostly saw couples who were in serious marital trouble. Often one or both of them came from unhappy families and needed help with basic skills. At the time I wrote my first book on this subject, I was primarily focused on the crises that kids provoked. I could get the couples through crises. But I wanted them to be really happy. And I also wanted my own marriage to be deeply happy and close, not merely polite.

I was married to a man who thought self-help books were possibly as good as paperweights. He would stare at me soulfully, promise to read them, and I would find them locked in the trunk of his car. Even though he was an avid reader of 900-plus page history books, he wasn't going to open a self-help book. He was, however, willing to proofread my first book, *Happily Married with Kids, It's Not Just A Fairy Tale,* about the normal stages couples go through and what helps them move through the various stages and crises.

Through the process, Neil and I both learned that a good marriage is one of the best gifts couples can give themselves and to all those around them. As our two boys are now both graduated from college, I am happy to report that Neil and I have become one of those genuinely happy couples I first noticed when this journey began. This is obviously one of the most rewarding things in life, and one of the main reasons I decided to revise my first book for this new edition.

Couples with step kids and gay couples with kids loved my first book. Turns out they were moving through the same stages and dealing with almost exactly the same issues themselves. Grandparents who had survived all the stages and achieved happiness wanted the book for their kids who were having first babies. I saw couples whose troubles started the same time they had kids but adored their kids and wouldn't dream of seeing their kids as a problem. And I eventually came to realize that even couples without kids move through the same stages and could benefit from the same advice.

As my coaching practice expanded, I got people before they had kids who were starting second relationships and found themselves getting stuck again in old patterns or who feared a repeat and wanted to learn to get it better this time. I had couples with both partners from divorced families who were scared and wanted to get it right the first time.

I also learned about attachment and the secret to a long-term sense of belonging together, no matter how different you may be. I learned you could be deeply in love or regain the experience of being soul mates even after the crisis of an emotional or physical affair. This was exciting stuff and gave me real hope that my clients could develop deep marital happiness. I wanted a guide that would help any couple stuck in these early painful stages but wanted to work for true, sustained, authentic happiness together.

Do you find yourselves having the same arguments that seem to emerge in predictable ways until you just stop talking, start yelling or simply give up? If so, you are ready for this book. Reading this will help you understand how to get happier with yourself and closer with your partner. This book shows how to take real, normal couple disagreements—even seemingly irresolvable issues—and use them as stepping stones to help you grow closer

This new book, *Happily Married With Kids, It's Not A Fairy Tale*, is a revised, updated edition of my first book. I have condensed the information, updated the references and added a chapter on dealing with tough economic times. As you read it, I hope you will laugh a little with me, nod in recognition and gain a clear vision of how a happy couple works and plays and even disagrees together as they grow closer.

.

Introduction: What Is Happening to Us?

Do you find yourselves having the same stupid arguments over and over again as your relationship circles down the drain? Would you like to learn how to turn those arguments into meaningful conversations that bring you closer?

Neil and I were married four years before having our first child, but soon after our son arrived, I began to wonder, "What happened to our marriage?" Before long, I found myself at the checkout stand in the store, reading magazine articles with titles like, "How to put romance back in your marriage," or "Is sex less fun?"

"Less," I thought, "they certainly got the less part right."

One article by a very famous sex therapist said, "Set aside time for sex and make it a priority…if you are tired, you are ambivalent about sex." When I first read this, I was standing in a checkout line, by now with *two* sons, each wrapped around one of my thighs. I thought, "Boy, I am always too tired for sex." And I certainly never used to be ambivalent about it!

Another article I read called having children the "antimatter of sex." And that wasn't the only pleasure I was missing. I missed long talks with my husband over dinner and movie marathons. We had so looked forward to having our kids. We were crazy about them. So what exactly was the problem?

Looking back, I can see that Neil and I were so wrapped up in the kids that we had no relationship. We lived in the same house but we rarely spent any time alone with each other. Our marriage wasn't even on the to-do list. Like most dedicated parents, we couldn't see the problem. We thought we were good parents and that that should be enough.

I started talking honestly about this issue to my friends and their husbands. One perceptive husband said there were times when he felt like he and his wife, who both had demanding careers, had become co-workers in the family business. He no longer felt a connection to his wife, no longer felt like best friends or certainly not like lovers, even though they had scheduled a "date" every Sunday morning at seven.

My clients with young kids felt the same disconnection from their spouses. Although by the time they came to me for therapy, they were often in serious trouble and ready to divorce. Couples in my practice who sought help with their marriage said that their problems started when their children were younger than five. In fact, having their second child intensified the problem or triggered the final meltdown. Other couples had kids but loved them so much that they couldn't imagine that had anything to do with the onset of their problems.

I found that children themselves are not the problem. It's the parents' reaction to the children that creates the problem.

Because they are focused on their children's needs, partners may miss the clues to this crisis. A new father may say, "You pay more attention to the baby than to me!" His wife may respond, "So what is your point? Babies need more attention."

"You pay more attention to the baby than me!"

In this exchange, each person missed the red flag—the opportunity to notice and then to address the anger that signaled a problem. To the husband, his statement may have felt like an admission of vulnerability, but to the wife, it probably sounded like he was criticizing or blaming her. His signal might have been easier to understand if he had said, "I miss my time with you." She could have responded to his need for attention by saying, "I miss you, too. What can we do about spending more time together?" But stress tends to make people irritable rather than reasonable. Irritability is like a small flame that can get fanned into a wildfire that grows and grows.

Often, parents don't realize that one of the best things they can give their children is a good marriage. Not only does it protect children from the obvious financial and emotional disruptions of divorce, a good marriage provides a role model for happiness, kindness, maintaining a sense of yourself in a group, and getting along with people in the world.

Through my research, I realized that my marital discomfort after having kids is typical. I also learned that because Neil and I were 40 and 39 when we became parents, we were at risk for a more intense crisis. It seems that the older you are when you start having kids—or the longer you are married before having children—the harder it is to adjust.

At the other end of the continuum, teenage couples and couples who had little time together before their babies arrived also have a very hard time. Couples in the middle range usually have an easier time, probably because they had good memories of their time spent together before having kids and had not yet settled into a comfortable rhythm (or more rigid rut?).

Part One

Baby on Board:

USING CHAOS TO CREATE COUPLE CLOSENESS

1 Baby Bliss Versus Baby Blues

Many parents are over-the-moon happy about their new baby. A first child adds a new excitement, a new kind of love and another dimension of meaning to their lives. Having a child tends to clarify, crystallize, or even capsize a person's ideas about what is important in life. Sudden changes in values and habits sometimes occur. Non-religious people get religious. Flexible people become rigid about eating schedules. Fearless people develop fears. Travelers refuse to travel. Dedicated career women sometimes decide to stop working. Sexually enthusiastic couples lose their sex drive.

Worse, partners sometimes assume that certain "natural" changes will occur in their spouses that just don't happen. For example, I assumed that after we had kids, Neil would naturally want to stay home more. But he still wanted to work ten- and twelve-hour days and still wanted to have us all run around on weekends. I was perplexed and exhausted. It is not unusual that conflict follows when spouses feel tricked or confused by the changes or lack of expected changes in their partners.

If the disappointment or differing expectations can be expressed, however, the conflict can be addressed directly and the problem more likely resolved. I could have said to Neil, "I'm really disappointed that you are still spending so much time at work. I had envisioned that we would spend more time as a family. I am curious, though, about what you pictured our life after kids would be like?" That could have started a discussion, which might have led to a clarification of our shared hopes for the family.

If each of the new parents' differing assumptions and expectations are addressed in a grumpy, critical way rather than tactfully, resentments accumulate over the first two to five years. As the child becomes more mobile and demanding and the history of resentments builds, parents feel more justified and "reasonable" expecting (and demanding) change in each other "for the sake of the child."

Often, the person requesting change is not aware that they want the change as much for themselves as for the child. For example, one parent might say to the other, "I want our kids to remember their Christmases at home, so let's not go to your parents' place this year."

EXPECTED STRUGGLES

Conflict in the first years of parenthood is expected and natural. According to one of my favorite authors, Harriet Lerner, in *The Mother Dance,* even when both parents make a deliberate effort to defy traditional gender arrangements, they are likely to struggle with six things:

1. Money (Mom has lost earning power; Dad has gained earning power.)
2. Childcare and housework (Mom notices and does more; she feels more responsible.)
3. Work outside the home (Dad's job comes first; he feels more responsible.)
4. Extended family issues (Mom over deals with his family and Dad under deals with his family.)
5. Sex (Mom becomes disinterested as the unequal distribution of domestic tasks takes its toll.)
6. Deciding how to spend what little free time the couple has together (Dad and Mom go out for the evening and argue about the previously mentioned items.)

While this may be a legitimate desire, sometimes the needs of the child get tangled up with the wishes of the parent, and sometimes a request for change may sound like a demand. Listen to how differently this request sounds rephrased:

"I think it is hard on all of us to travel at Christmas, and I want the kids to have memories of Christmas in our house with us. Do you have any ideas how we could accomplish that?" When couples get on the same side of a problem, things work out better.

Good friends of ours cleared work from their shared home desk one day by pitching all their papers over the balcony together with comical exaggerated accusations about having four children and no time. They howled with laughter when they told this story. As a semi-neat freak, I was horrified. But I realized it put them on the same side of the mess, making fun of their desire to blame each other and forcing them to clean up together rather than fight. Their sense of humor keeps them happily married.

From these examples, we see that deeper intimacy comes not from what we share by having children, but from how we resolve the many new conflicts and changes that children bring to our relationship. Problems become opportunities for intimacy and laughter.

Yet most couples don't see the opportunity for growing closer. Instead, partners see the conflict as failure. They do not see that intimacy is an accomplishment couples literally fight for (and work for) by resolving the inevitable disappointments and savoring the moments of happiness that come with their children. Couples aren't pre-programmed for greater intimacies as I had erroneously assumed; they must create it for themselves.

One valuable set of expectations from before kids (BK) does not change for happily married couples with kids:

Happy couples maintain a certain standard of civility or caring, a set of unwritten rules about not hurting too deeply or irreparably, or allowing themselves to be hurt too deeply during their conflict. After a fight or discussion they can reconnect and respect each other again.

Happy couples disagree and set limits with each other in ways that leave each person's self-respect intact. In fact, research suggests that couples don't last when the husband can't indicate "disgust" or displeasure with a plan or action. Happy couples know that it is not whether you disagree that matters, because you will, but how you work things out.

Happy couples resolve the demands of parenting in many fascinating ways. The following chapters are filled with normal conflicts and the ways that couples resolve them to create happiness in their marriage.

Happy couples make relaxed time for sharing sex, affection and fun.

EXPECTATIONS VERSUS REALITIES

Here are the five core fantasies paired with a dose of reality. Your experiences may not always fall neatly into these categories. Some couples manage to feel all five disappointments acutely, while others may focus on only one or two. You may add a few new ones of your own.

WE EXPECT:

- **Tender Family Time:** We'll have many tender moments together at home with a cooing baby.
- **Closer Soul Mates:** We will share all the fun we had before but have even more in common after the baby.
- **Continued Equality:** Our relationship will be more equal than our parents' marriage was.
- **Support:** We will be one another's main emotional and practical support.
- **Our Family/New Start:** We'll do things better than our parents and make up for things we missed.

WE GET:

- **The Red-Eye Special:** Sleep deprivation, crankiness, irritability, less—not more—quality time and falling asleep in tender moments.
- **Unexpected Differences:** Children change us in unexpected ways. Each partner experiences parenthood differently.
- **Tag Team Parenting:** A new workload and a new definition of fairness.
- **Community:** We learn "It takes a village to raise a parent."
- **Ghosts from the Past:** Finding out our past can powerfully disrupt the present.

Tips for Tender Couple and Family Time

Couple Time

Time alone as a couple is high priority. This time makes a marriage strong. Carve out two kinds of time together: time to just "date," for fun and romance with little serious talk, and time I call "staff time" to organize for the family needs. Make this "staff time" independent of your date time so you don't spend date time battling about parenting or doing routine problem solving. Daily, weekly and quarterly times are important. Successful couples often have some combination of all three.

Couple Daily Time

Happy couples make regular time for each other in different ways. There is no one right way to make time.

- Some couples have telephone-free time each day together.
- Some have 20 minutes together in bed either early in the morning or late in the evening while kids are sleeping.

- Some take walks before breakfast or after dinner. These walks are wonderful when you have an infant but as kids become more verbal you will need to find a new time that is just yours.
- Some people romance each other via e-mail during the day.
- Rare couples commute together or have lunch together regularly.
- I know long-distance couples who have regular Skype dates.

Whatever your plan, you *need* this time to stay connected. It was interesting to me that 20 minutes seemed to be the time most often mentioned by satisfied couples.

Couple Weekly Time: M. A. D.

This tip to *Make A Date* is so important that I will repeat it frequently throughout the book. When you see M.A.D., know that it stands for *Make A Date or you and your partner will end up MAD at each other much too often.*

- Successful couples often have a standing date with a babysitter one night a week. Couples see this as especially necessary before kids are four.
- Some couples go out right after work on a weeknight so they don't have to say good-by to the kids twice. Having regular family time the day before or the afternoon before date time alleviates parenting guilt and makes the date go better.
- Many people think of childcare as something they need so they can go to work but they don't see it as something they need for their marriage.

Quarterly and Yearly Couple Time:

Some couples wait for a marital crisis before they schedule their first overnight or long day or evening away from the kids. A better approach is to schedule trips to prevent crises.

- One couple plans an anniversary overnight every year.

- Another couple does Valentine's overnight once a year. They make the reservation for next year when they check out.
- Some couples have a 'staycation' or getaway each quarter.
- When kids are older, some happy couples balance couple and family time with a 3-day or week-long parent vacation once a year while the kids visit grandparents, stay with friends, or go to camp.

As we discuss later, these first trips are often a source of conflict and must be planned carefully, taking into consideration the age of the child and the issues of the parents. I know several happy couples who didn't schedule a trip alone until the kids were 10, but had such great daily and weekly habits for connecting that they felt very close.

Family Time

Good family time makes the time you spend away as a couple better because you feel connected and happy in your relationship with your kids. Though kids can't help much at first, the time you take with them to do small tasks and just be together pays big benefits later.

Daily Family Time:

Many studies show that families who consistently have a meal together each day have healthier and better performing kids in school and life.

- Breakfast works as well as dinner as family connection time.
- Some heroic parents get up for work at 4 or 5 a.m. to be home for dinner.
- Others change their jobs to shorten or eliminate a commute.
- Kids also need one-on-one times with at least one parent each day. Time alone with each parent is better. Ten to 20 minutes of positive time before dinner or bed with each child makes a big difference.

- Consider *not answering the phone during meals and/or for an hour at bedtime.* Both kids and partners are frustrated by interruptions. Imagine how you feel when a movie is interrupted. When you don't answer the phone, children get the message that they are very important to you. Friends and family adjust to this schedule quickly, especially if you tell them why you are doing it.

Weekly Family Time:

Families need both fun time and "teamwork time" when the family pulls together and plans or works. Make sure you have both.

- Create "just our family" time, like Sunday nights for a special meal and games, movies or songs.
- Plan Saturday morning chores/errands time. Designate a family day or a family evening. For one night a week, let the machine get the phone and don't answer the door.
- Later we discuss family meetings for older kids.
- When kids are older, even though friends are almost always welcome, set aside "just our family time" for special times and for intense discussions about rules and responsibilities.

Couples say this tradition or habit works at all ages of children's lives. Family activities will change when kids are five versus10, but the togetherness is what's important. I have known both an insurance executive and a real-estate broker who took every Wednesday off because they had been gone on weekends so much when the kids were young. Both have great relationships with both their spouses and their kids, and are in the top 1 percent in their field in earnings. That Wednesday became a symbol to all of them that family was a priority. They only wish they had done it sooner.

Quarterly and Yearly Family Time:

Weekends and family vacations create memories that hold the family together. Some vacation time needs to be "just our family" if you want to foster a feeling of family closeness. However, vacations and weekends with family friends are great fun for kids and parents. They teach kids (and parents) a lot.

- Some couples have an annual camping trip with other young families.
- Another group plans to donate time in an orphanage for a weekend once a year.
- Some families create memories with a vacation destination each summer at grandparents or with family and cousins.
- Some do a family getaway at the beach or the mountains.
- Some go traveling or camping as "just our family."
- Some take best friends.
- Some go to family reunions.
- Some enjoy action adventures such as family camp.

These activities are fun to look forward to and to plan at the weekly meetings we will discuss later.

BABY BLUES By Rick Kirkman and Jerry Scott

2 The New Parent Bond

New parents may expect to grow closer to each other because of the baby, but the reality is that having a new baby is disruptive and exhausting. In the beginning, couples may take long walks together while the baby is in the backpack or stroller. Unfortunately, these times fuel expectations that soon won't be met. Most young couples, even those with hideously stressful schedules, have far more uninterrupted talk time and fun time together before kids than they will for many years after the baby arrives. Each partner vies for the hour or two of "free" time that is rarely enough to get the necessities of family life handled, much less allow for personal time, time with friends or the extra hour needed at work. Going to the grocery store by yourself may be as good as it gets some weeks.

Now that she is home more Mom may fantasize that she will work on all those creative projects she had put aside earlier. Dad may fantasize that now that Mom is home more, she will take his clothes to the dry cleaners, take over bill paying, and be home when he gets there. One parent's dream may be a little different from the other's. Yet, both feel frustrated, as less, not more gets done.

Bottles and toys encroach on personal space and routines are disrupted. Mom may feel she doesn't deserve to go shopping or hire help because she is making less money. She may feel frustrated and isolated because no one is listening to her or asking her opinion as they used to at work. Because she is staying home, she may not ask for or expect her husband's help, and thus she grows more exhausted.

With less income, Dad may be fearful they won't meet the bills, let alone fill the retirement account and college funds.

Focused on these concerns, he may feel they do not have the money for a getaway dinner or weekend away. Mom may not be ready to leave the baby for fear of interrupting the bonding or because she likes to be available to the baby.

When both parents work, the shelter of work can serve to divide the couple even more. For some parents, especially as the child moves out of infancy and into toddling and talking, work becomes a welcome relief from the constant demands of a two-year-old. If they work in separate places or mom remains at home, the quiet retreat of the workplace separates them more from each other.

> *...repetitive arguments about closeness, jealousy, and time spent are really about the raw spots we bring to the relationship from early childhood and previous relationships....*

Baffled by all this, parents sense their reality falls far short of their dreams. They love their kids more than they could have imagined and focus their attention there, not on each other. As a result, compromise and expediency become the order of the day. Time alone or at work and family—which needs to become a priority—is set aside. Everyone compromises couple time and all feel resentful.

The silver lining to all this disruption is that it can provide a venue for solid and joyful parental bonding. Sue Johnson, (described by couples researcher John Gottman as the best marital therapist in the world—and I would have to agree) outlines seven essential conversations for a strong marital bond in her 2008 book, *Hold Me Tight*. The mini-crises of new parenthood provide just the fuel to create an even stronger bond between parents. Her book comes in audio format so that busy new parents can listen while commuting or exercising.

The first conversation is about recognizing your Demon Dialogues, the same repetitive, ugly, frustrating fights. She encourages couples to name their "crazy arguments"—the ones that you have over and over again that leave each of you feeling angry, misunderstood and frustrated. Sue says all these fights are about being able to depend on each other emotionally, ask for help with emotional issues, and feel as if your partner cares how you feel and has your back. The arrival of children stirs up numerous emotional issues that we will describe in upcoming chapters, so the likelihood for having repetitive painful arguments is great. Men often feel inadequate when asked to provide emotional support. Women tend to feel cut off and desperate, although, of course, depending on your childhood history, these roles can be reversed.

The second conversation is simply to identify those raw spots together when they happen. Being able to stop and say, "This is a crummy replay of an argument we have all the time," allows you to take a new direction. Recognizing there are deeper feelings underneath that need attention allows you to problem solve and implement workable solutions. Saying "Let's take a break and start over," is about joining each other on the same side against your fights.

She believes that the underlying issue in repetitive arguments about closeness, jealousy, and time spent are really about the raw spots we bring to the relationship from early childhood and previous relationships, and even unresolved issues from this relationship.

The third kind of essential conversation requires us to go back and relive rocky moments together and find out exactly what you did or said that was upsetting and hurtful to your partner and have you hear what your partner was feeling and vice versa. We will talk about this in the chapter on "healed by listening" (chapter 18).

The fourth conversation leads to real bonding and to preventing future demon dialogues (or death dances as I sometimes call them). In these conversations, partners practice having one partner ask for emotional support and having the other respond and engage in listening, and then feeding back what they hear. Each partner needs to be able to experience this "asking for" and then getting a response and support.

I often ask clients if they can ask for a hug. If they cannot ask for a hug in the relationship, then I strongly suspect they have issues that need to be explored. Asking for and receiving a hug is a mini-model of being able to ask for and get a response and emotional support.

The fifth conversation involves learning how to forgive injuries and get over things. Partners will disappoint each other regularly in a marriage. With children, the opportunities to disappoint multiply exponentially. So it is essential to learn how to forgive and move on with a better plan for next time. Learning to both apologize and forgive in a meaningful, satisfying way strengthens the marital bond. Although the basic process is simple, many couples develop unique fun ways to do this. We will talk about excellent apologies later.

In the sixth conversation you address sex and touch. New moms are often overwhelmed and very engaged in all the touching with a young child. Dad feels left out. I discuss this thoroughly in the chapter on sex. I strongly agree with Sue that sex can actually improve throughout a marriage and doesn't necessarily or naturally decline. Using the changes in feelings about sex that normally occur when children are small, you can create better communication and lay the groundwork for a happier and healthier sex life for the rest of your life.

The seventh conversation helps you communicate with each other to have a long-term happy connection. The mark of happy, healthy, vibrant relationships is flexibility and adaptability as family and partner needs change. Another of her books, *Emotionally Focused Couple Therapy with Trauma Survivors: Strengthening Attachment Bonds*, addresses how a good marriage helps heal normal childhood issues and the more major traumas that each person brings to the marriage. As your marital connection grows and your healing continues, over time your relationship will become warmer, more fun, and more meaningful.

When my kids were young, I often read child-rearing books over and over when I felt myself slipping into old bad habits with my kids. I would encourage you to read or listen to Sue's book on audio several times throughout your marriage, as it may have more meaning as time passes.

Sue Johnson's work is the most well-researched and effective marital therapy today. In 12 to 20 ninety-minute sessions, most couples can get their relationship repaired and sail smoothly into their future. Relatively high functioning couples can do it in eight, or they can read her book, *Hold Me Tight*. Emotion-Focused Therapy, or EFT, is one of a very few therapies that help you continue getting better when therapy ends. You can go the EFT website to find therapists who specialize in EFT.

THE RED-EYE SPECIAL: SLEEP DISRUPTION

Our friend, Bill, described his lovely and cheerful wife, Maria, as a "Pit Viper" without adequate sleep. In other couples we knew, although more rarely, the dad could not function without regular sleep. I noticed, as my girlfriends' kids arrived, their idea of a dream vacation shifted from Tahiti with their man to sleeping in any clean, quiet hotel room alone.

Sleep deprivation causes moderate to severe problems for 30 to 50 percent of new parents. Mothers often report never sleeping as soundly after the arrival of their first child. This lack of sound sleep may not feel like a problem at first, but often becomes more severe and chronic as the child grows. In addition, sleep deprivation—either not enough sleep or constant sleep interruption—often inhibits sexual desire and/or causes frequent headaches, irritability, and even poor judgment.

Sleep deprivation may create great conflict between partners. If the less affected partner can't tolerate the irritability of the more sleep-deprived partner, the situation becomes worse. The deprived partner may come to feel that sleep is his/her most important survival need, an absolute necessity, and critical to family survival that they be able to function at work. The person requiring sleep is often viewed as selfish by the one who isn't as tired and irritable, even though studies show that sleep deprivation can cause a measurable drop in neurotransmitters and thus a significant depression.

Sometimes couples argue about the "right" amount of sleep a person should require rather than accepting they have different sleep needs. Other couples argue who needs it most. Successful couples make a plan that realistically accommodates both parents' sleep needs and accept that kids will disrupt both the sleep and the plan frequently. Many good books on this subject are listed in resources on my website.

Good Sense for Good Sleep

There are two very divergent views of how to get children to sleep well. Richard Ferber, author of *Solve Your Child's Sleep Problems*, recommends a number of strategies that involve putting children down for naps and bedtime and letting them cry it out. His recommendations are more sophisticated than I describe here and vary with the age of the child. His most vociferous critics usually have not read his book. Many tender-hearted parents haven't got the heart for this approach, however.

Conversely, Dr. William Sears advocates the family bed approach also known as attachment parenting. Discussed in the books of Katie Granju and Tine Thevenin, this approach suggests that children sleep in the same bed with parents until they spontaneously give it up sometime before puberty, (or college?!) So what is a reasonable parent to do?

Research in the personality development of children reared under either extreme method is nonexistent, though both approaches appear to have adherents with happily married couples and reasonably well-functioning children. Some critics of the family bed approach have suggested that while it seemed to work well for the kids, it led to the end of their marriage. The Ferber followers teach parents to hang tough while their kids cry, so parents have time alone in their marital bed and kids can learn the important skill of falling asleep alone. The family bed people schedule sex and intimate talk time outside the bedroom, on vacation or at different times of the day. With a little common sense, parents and kids can reap the benefits of both approaches. But the reality is, your kids will learn to sleep through the night and occasionally your kids will be waking you up at night right through college.

To develop a plan that works for you and your spouse, consider both the developmental stage of your child and your own needs as parents. Clearly, if you insist your child be allowed to scream and your partner feels that letting the child scream is child abuse, you won't be getting much sex anyway! Likewise, if your partner requires eight to nine hours of uninterrupted sleep to be a civil human being, the family bed will cause family discord and/or distance. So what is the golden mean?

I advocate helping the baby become familiar with different ways of falling asleep. In infancy, you can comfort an infant by keeping a reasonably stable schedule of nap and bed times but slightly different routines. Sometimes put them down in the bed or crib when they are sleepy and let them go to sleep. Sometimes rock them to sleep.

Nursing infants are often comfortably kept in bed with mom if she is a light sleeper and prefers it. Other parents start the baby in a crib by the bed and transfer the baby into bed for nursing and then return them to the crib. Nursing at night and diaper changes are best done with the lights off or very low and as little stimulation as possible unless you are a night owl and want to party with junior regularly in the middle of the night.

By three months and definitely prior to nine months, the baby should transition to sleeping outside the family bed, if you want this as a predominant pattern during childhood. Giving the baby a clear routine at bedtime that includes a bath, play time, a story, a song and lights out is a common method. Such a routine needs to take into account the natural talents and inclinations of the family. My son at age one-and-a-half clearly announced more than once, "Don't sing, just rock!"

The obvious trick that most books don't tell you is to vary who carries out this bedtime routine. If mom and dad and occasionally a beloved caretaker take turns, your child will be more flexible after nine months, accepting either of you or the baby sitter. A healthy baby will have learned some valuable self-comforting skills for getting back to sleep without parental intervention. Having a good, portable, washable "transition object" like a bear, a bunny or a blankie or something with the parental scent available at bed times helps.

Right around nine months most kids start waking up and babbling or screaming in their own beds. They are too young to talk, but old enough to know that if they scream you will run to their side. Since I require a lot of sleep, I was horrified when my son, Xander, began doing this at nine months after sleeping very soundly for the first eight or so. (Neil says I have delusional hormones that make Xander's sleep seem better than it was.) I read all about the family bed and Ferber's approach. I couldn't bring myself to let Xander scream and I needed my sleep too much to have a kicker in bed with us. My husband, who sleeps through California earthquakes, supported whatever method I chose. After three weeks of thorough reading and big dark circles under my eyes, I met a mom in the park who said she suffered for seven months before she tried Ferber's method of having them cry it out. Armed with this single testimony and desperation, I put a little red glow-in-the-dark alarm clock by my bed and I promised myself I would lie there for five minutes after the crying started before I went in.

When he woke up and howled, I clutched the glowing face of the alarm and watched the seconds tick. He cried for less than two minutes and didn't scream again at night—ever. What a relief!

I was lucky. My mentor from the park said her kid screamed for 15 minutes the first time and for a few more nights before he gave it up for good. Two weeks is a more normal time to adjust to a new routine. Since my children struggled with this, I found a wonderful book that addresses this middle-of-the-road solution for your child: *The No-Cry Sleep Solution: Gentle Ways to Help Your Baby Sleep Through the Night* by Elizabeth Pantley. I highly recommend it. She also has books about toddlers and napping.

Some parents make *the transition with older kids* by cuddling on the bed for a while and then saying I will come back in a few minutes, after I brush my teeth or let the dog out or some other friendly excuse. They then disappear and return, without being asked, a few times until the child drifts off. Most children want to know you are available more than they need your constant presence. I found my children were more likely to wake us if we had not been there to cuddle a little before they went to sleep. As children grow older they understand simple explanations like, "If you wake Mommy in the night just to talk, then she is really cranky the next day and we all have a bad time."

Angela, a creative friend of mine with three kids, began piano lessons. After comforting each child individually, it was her practice time. She established a routine of playing classical music softly for them to hear from their rooms as they drifted off to sleep. She improved while her kids grew. I didn't have the talent or the stamina for that, but I loved the idea. Her kids all play musical instruments now.

The point is that you can both comfort your children and get them sleeping well in their own beds. Start early and vary your routine. Have more than one person put them to bed. Letting young children fall asleep on your bed or their bed while you rub their back is okay as long as they can fall asleep in both places, so that when they are too big to carry they still have a comforting ritual. Accept that this process is imperfect and will fall apart when they are sick.

If your children have special needs, night terrors, or you can't get them sleeping alone in their own beds, talk to other mothers or professionals. Regardless, work out a way with your partner that allows you each to take good care of your kids and also have tender times for just the two of you.

3 Can We Stay Best Friends?

Couples believe a baby will be a new, common interest that will bring them closer as soul mates. The reality is that men and women change and grow in different directions and in ways they never expected.

Differences in experience begin with pregnancy. For many women, pregnancy brings nausea, fatigue, swollen ankles, and other discomforts not usually mentioned in mixed company. Even if a woman loves pregnancy and is perfectly healthy, the sheer weight gain and the rioting hormones cause any woman to slow down and turn her thoughts inward. People begin to react to a pregnant woman differently. For some women, each task she performs while moving around like a hippo raises questions about how this baby will change her life.

Men, on the other hand, often begin to focus on making money or career advancement. If a man doesn't focus on this spontaneously, he often feels a not-so-subtle social pressure to do so. "Have you started that college fund, yet?" people joke. But the point is not lost. He may panic about money. He may think about what kind of model of career success and status he will be for his child. Even when the man has a well-established career, he may decide that the birth of his child signals a time to expand or change directions.

Even the most independent women find pregnancy is a period of surprising emotional dependency. Mom may crave reassurance that she is attractive, feel very physically and emotionally vulnerable, and want extra help with decisions and duties. For most couples, the fact that the wife can burst into tears over a funny look upsets both the woman's sense of herself and the man's sense of her independence. How the couple handles this period of emotional dependency can set the tone for the rest of the relationship. Several women reported to me that they never regained their early sense of self-assertion after their first child and this led to great unhappiness in the marriage.

This sense of dependency can be a special strain on a relationship if, for example, the wife experienced an early trauma involving dependency. Women who were punished as children for normal dependency needs as a child or had a parent abandon the family often experience significant difficulties later during their pregnancies. In either of these cases, the new mom might be unable to talk about or accept that she feels very dependent. She can become quite critical of her partner's efforts to be supportive or she might withdraw completely in anticipation of being abandoned.

Likewise, if the husband was required to be an emotional caretaker for his mother, he can be quite upset by his wife's new needs. He can feel like, "I married her because she was independent and now it turns out she is not!" Clear communication of respect and an understanding that the dependency is temporary leads to closeness and a positive outcome. If either Dad or Mom had difficulty or issues with normal dependency needs, the change in their relationship may feel emotionally unsafe. People who feel unsafe avoid sex, and problems ensue.

However, when the new mother is encouraged to talk about her sensitivity and feeling of dependency and the new father enjoys being (or is guided to be) supportive, attentive and nurturing, she experiences her partner as responsive and supportive. He experiences her as appreciative. Together they can both feel more secure, knowing that as things change, they can both adapt and be there for each other.

As one woman described it, "It felt like a huge leap of faith. For the first time I really needed my husband. I think I liked knowing that and I got better about trusting since he came through so well. Very scary though."

BABY BLUES By Rick Kirkman and Jerry Scott

After the first child arrives, these differences between men and women intensify. Whether adoption, bottle-feeding, or breast-feeding is involved, Mom, not Dad, usually takes off several months or more from work to bond with the new baby.

As one comedian quipped about the night after the arrival of his baby, "Ever notice how when a baby arrives, men suddenly become useless around the house?" In fact, a new dad is often treated like an idiot. Frequently, the arrival of the child means that his mother and his mother–in-law are around more. Men tell me that having their wife, mother, and mother-in-law all giving sometimes wildly contradictory advice and detailed "suggestions" is intimidating and humiliating. These women are eager to share knowledge and may not see themselves as humiliating anyone. The new mom is often in an experimental mode and excited to share what seems to be working for her baby. In turn, she may seem as if she is more sure of herself than she actually feels. This enthusiasm creates even more distance between the new mom and dad.

Typically, new dads are treated in ways that tend to drive them out of their marriage and into their cave. Whether that cave is golf, a garage workshop, or the computer, when mistreated, most dads retreat to an emotional safety zone and away from talk and intimacy.

When Mom finally does decide to let Dad step in and take care of the kids, it is a set up for failure. No way can Dad step into the parenting and housekeeping job and do it as well as an experienced Mom. He is even less likely to do it the way she wants. She is likely to compare his attempts unfavorably to other mothers or childcare workers. The regular childcare provider is probably around kids all the time and understands her baby's habits and sensitivities, causing Mom to wonder why Dad is so out of it.

When you are around children a lot, you hone the habits that insure a smoother day, such as pushing glasses to the center of the table so that they are not accidentally knocked off. People who are around children for many hours a day understand the penalty for disrupted routines, like a missed snack or nap. Since Dad may not be around kids as much, he may tend to celebrate by letting them skip naps and stay up late. This can bring chaos and a rain of criticism from Mom.

Some clever fellows develop a charming cultivated incompetence, which both flatters Mom and avoids the work. "Oh, you do the sunscreen so much better than I do" (or "sun scream," as some harried parents call it). The sad result is that he both excludes himself from a connection with his child and burdens his wife. Don't fall for it. Have a sense of humor and dish it right back, "You are such a fast learner, I know you will catch on with a little practice! Besides, they love attention from their daddy."

When you are around children a lot, you hone the habits that insure a smoother day, such as pushing glasses to the center of the table so that they are not accidentally knocked off.

If Mom does all of the child rearing herself, she is cutting her husband out of some important connections with his child and important parent-to-parent sharing. This is the weakness of the traditional mom-does-it-all model. If she does everything herself, career or no career, she will very likely not be able to both raise her kids and stay in tune with her spouse. The marriages of the '50s and '60s were functional, not intimate. This is precisely the period that spawned the women's movement. Many children raised in the '50s and '60s say they felt cut off from their fathers. Mothers and children became isolated in a world of other mothers and children. Moms and dads were cut off from each other. Excluding Dad, by his choice or not, is everyone's loss.

Today, some moms may be unable to let their husbands help because they need to justify staying at home. Others, who felt neglected as kids themselves, want so much to get their mothering right that they can't let Dad help. She is trying to heal herself as she cares for the kids.

It would be better to let Dad spend time fathering and make some "mistakes." Even when Mom doesn't work outside the home, kids need time alone with Dad. Spouses will feel more connected and share more experiences if they each take time alone caring for the kids. Laughing together about childrearing glitches works better than living in two very separate worlds.

Women often see men as simply not understanding what needs to be done and just not helping enough. Men, missing their wives, try to rekindle romance and excitement, often before their partner is psychologically ready.

I remember when Neil surprised me with tickets for a fabulous10-day vacation in Switzerland for a friend's wedding. It sounds wonderful, right? Well, not exactly. The tickets were nonrefundable. The vacation fell during the first week of my teaching schedule at the university. And I had to leave my three- and four-year-old boys with Neil's mom, followed by lots of jumping on and off trains. Instead of feeling rested and romantic, I felt like a tin can tied to the tail of a labrador retriever. I would have loved this vacation pre-kids, and I will probably love a vacation like this again when we have an empty nest. But I didn't love it then. I felt guilty about leaving work and my kids. I missed the kids badly. I needed some rest. I complained a lot. Moreover, I felt misunderstood since he didn't share my guilt about leaving the kids. Neil was great. He listened. At least we had plenty of time during that vacation to figure out what was so wrong for me. Ultimately, we decided that while the kids were small, we wouldn't have any more surprise vacations. Instead, we would sort out our priorities and make plans together.

Most couples experience conflicts similar to the ones I have described even when Mom doesn't work outside the home. The husband wants to have fun and reconnect the way they used to, and the wife is worried about the babysitter and the house. Sometimes, the reverse occurs, the wife is the one missing the fun and the husband, who's at work a lot, misses the kids and doesn't want to leave home. The danger to the marriage is that the wife begins to doubt her love for her partner because she is less excited about doing things together. The romantic husband feels unloved because the new mom is always saying no to his invites. Other moms would see her refusal as understandable. Quite often a mom fantasizes about getting away by herself without Dad or kids, something she never would have considered pre-kids. These feelings may also make both of them wonder if the marriage is failing. So talking about and accepting these concerns as normal can make them feel like best friends again and can lay the groundwork for wanting to spend time alone together again.

SNORING

After the birth of the first child, snoring is a remarkably common issue for already sleep-deprived couples, and it tests a couple's negotiating and cooperating skills! Mom sleeps more lightly now, listening for the baby. Maybe her hormones change so she can hear more acutely, but I doubt it. The dad's snoring or her own may awaken her, disrupting sleep even more. Of course, in some couples, Dad gets up with the baby and experiences this problem. In either case, the discovery of what sounds like a dying seal in your bed is disconcerting. There are many solutions, most of which Neil and I have tried.

- **Separate bedrooms:** Mom may move out of the bedroom occasionally. This is a practical move with obvious problems for the relationship. Dad thinks they will never have sex again. Paradoxically, if Mom requests Dad to sleep elsewhere and he agrees, she may then feel both relieved and then abandoned. Talking about this and having snuggling or together time before you sleep elsewhere helps.

- **Earplugs:** When the baby grows enough to get out of the crib and come tug on your sleeve when he or she is ill or needs you, or if your partner will wake when the child calls for help, the newer soft gel earplugs work very well. I trained myself to sleep with a pillow over my head and face to muffle sound but it isn't a solution I recommend.
- **Snoring Cures:** With a vested interest in this problem, I discovered many purported cures.
- Breathing strips that attach to your nose,
- eliminating alcohol prior to bedtime,
- nutritional supplements available at health food stores called SNORE,
- even a mist you can spray in your husbands face that promises not to wake him up,
- dental plates that position the jaw,
- losing weight, evaluation for sleep apnea, and
- surgery are all solutions that work for some people some of the time.

A snorer often has trouble accepting any of these solutions (except earplugs) since he or she may have been cheerfully snoring for many years without complaint. The snorer usually views the complaints with mild bemusement or disbelief. The snoring cures may seem personally intrusive, critical, and unnecessarily extreme. The snorer is also not desperate from sleep deprivation and therefore lacks empathy. The light sleeper can grow quite resentful and enraged if the snorer ignores the complaints or treats them lightly. Mock suffocation by pillow may result. If your non-snorer moves out of the bedroom the problem is serious for him/her. Try to keep some perspective as a couple. This is only one of many mundane problems you get to share after kids. Work on a solution together and be very grateful if you don't have this problem.

Tips for Fostering Connection and Closeness

- Use your uninterrupted 20 minutes each day face-to-face talking and maybe cuddling, but, most importantly, listening to anything the other wants to say. Yes, when you are desperate, you can break it into two 10-minute chunks.
- Be curious, not furious, about differences. Don't try to persuade your partner to see differences logically, rationally, reasonably or your way. For two minutes, just listen. Then repeat back what you understand. Check your accuracy. Build up to 10 minutes.
- Take turns talking about what your fantasies for life with kids would be like.
- Talk about what you want for your marriage.
- Share when you feel the most love and pride in your child. When do you each enjoy your child the most? What is the hardest for each of you?
- Share what you each want for your kids. Write it down and save it. It is fun to revisit these lists and see how they change in light of who your child becomes.
- Keep a list of best and worst moments in parenting to laugh about together.
- Take a parenting class together. Neil says you will love it and be the only guy there.
- Talk about the kind of parent you want to be. Parenting issues aren't romantic but they are much more fun when you feel like you are on the same team.
- Read or listen to the same parenting or marriage book. (Who has time to read?)
- Create a time once a week to sit down and iron out scheduling difficulties, resolve division of labor issues, review childcare and make dates. Share one of the joint calendars on the Internet, sync PDAs, or use a simple wall calendar.
- Talk together about what a good couple relationship means to each of you.

- Talk about what time and other commitments you each need to make to fulfill your dreams.
- *Celebrate what you have.* Include compliments to your partner and good news about your kids and your day in every mini planning or sharing session.

4 The Mommy Dilemma

Stay home, go back to work, or try to ride with one foot on each horse? Being a mother is probably a woman's central identity, regardless of whether or not she works or how powerful or prestigious her work is. For the most part, a man's central identity is his work, not being a dad.

Indeed, it may be harder today to have a marriage and kids than it was a generation or two ago because so many more moms work. Most women with children younger than five now work at least part-time and the percentage of working mothers is rising. Full-time career moms obviously have a lot on their plate and studies repeatedly indicate they tend to be chronically sleep deprived. The part-time mom is trying to do some of everything and often feels the strongest pull between these two different worlds.

A full-time mom is often set up for exhaustion too. She may set very high expectations. She doesn't hire help, she doesn't initially ask her partner for help, and she doesn't give herself much-needed breaks. Twenty-four/seven has new meaning because routine time-off and breaks are not scheduled. Reality doesn't match the expectations and Mom becomes depleted.

The perception that staying home with kids isn't a real job aggravates the problem of balancing the new workload between the two parents. Dad may come home and sit down to read the paper, not recognizing that Mom needs him to take the baby, NOW! He may not recognize how exhausting her day has been since she has been "home all day." He thinks she has had all those great moments playing with the baby, which he missed while he was working hard for the family. She thinks he got adult conversation and lunch at a restaurant while she didn't get to shower until 3:00. In addition, she may become quite angry if he must work late or meet social obligations for work that interfere with his being home. Both partners are frustrated because they are doing their hard jobs well and want sympathy, appreciation, and a break. Instead, each partner envies the other's "freedom" and nobody gets a break.

If Dads would truly consider whether or not they would be willing to give up their jobs to take care of Junior and depend on Mom's income, or consider how they would be treated at work if they worked part-time, they might begin to appreciate the difficulty of the decision each mother makes. Often men who lose a job temporarily become paralyzed with depression. However, both partners may just expect that a woman gives up her job or career temporarily and cheerfully—sometimes repeatedly—to accommodate the needs of her husband and/or children. This has very real economic consequences. One man said that his wife used to be his boss. Now, after staying home with their child, she makes only a quarter of what he does. At least they felt close because he understood her sacrifice.

CATHY By Cathy Guisewite

5 Separate and Equal

Couples expect their relationship to stay relatively equal when a baby arrives, but the reality is that babies are the great *un*equalizers. Even prepared childbirth classes foster this expectation that there will be a lot of shared activity and involvement after the birth of the child.

If couples start out as equal career achievers, as many do, both are used to thinking of being at home as a break from their career rather than a demanding stressful setting after the child arrives. As a result, both are likely to underestimate the work needed to keep the home going once children arrive. Once you have kids, coming home from work takes on a whole new meaning. The inequality of the demands of the career and home situation often unfolds because initially women are eager to do a good job mothering. They take over the 24-hour childcare duties enthusiastically. Men cooperate. Both perpetuate the roles that they saw their parents assume. So, neither partner thinks about the consequences of this unequal arrangement for the long-term happiness of the marriage.

The fact is that women and men start with different notions about what equal parenting is, based on their parents' behavior during their own childhoods. Men look at their dads and say, "I am doing way more than he did if I do diapering once in a while." A new dad may feel quite generous about what he is contributing. Meanwhile, a new mom is thinking, "I am doing less than my mom did, but way more than my husband is doing, and way more than I can manage."

Several research studies on work distribution in the home show that although both partners do more work after the baby arrives, most men actually do a smaller share of the total workload. If both partners work outside the home, mom typically comes home to 275 percent more of the childcare and 15 percent more of the housework than her partner. Sounds like a mistake, right? Unfortunately it is not.

If Mom also works, both she and her husband may enjoy and depend on the money she makes. So he encourages her to work, and she may not see leaving her job as an option. Sadly, according to researchers, moms who work more than 35 hours a week also get less sleep than men and stay-at-home moms.

The overload and imbalance go hand in hand. Mom and Dad both incorrectly assume that a little outside help with childcare and cleaning will completely solve the overload and imbalance. While outside help is great, it doesn't usually solve the imbalance between the two parents.

Another complication occurs when Dad is an experienced parent with a child from a previous marriage and only reluctantly agreed to have this child. This piece of history often prevents Mom from asking for help until she is so overwhelmed that suddenly she is demanding help. Dad now feels even more unappreciated since he expressed his reluctance to take on the extra work from the outset.

To get back to a comfortable give and take that supports the growth of the marriage and the children, the couple needs to make some thoughtful decisions. Both partners must consider their expectations about what must be done, whether to get more help, define their roles more clearly, and/or negotiate compromises around issues of career and family. Yet faced with these big decisions, their problem-solving styles are likely to be very different.

Men are taught to emphasize negotiation while women are trained in cooperation. A woman may say, "I need help with the kids. I am exhausted." She would like— or perhaps expect— him to ask, "How can I help?" But a man might think, "You want to share chores? Sure, let's negotiate." His point of view is, "Why volunteer for trouble?" at the beginning of a negotiation. So, he says, cheerfully or defensively, "I'll take out the trash." And, he expects his wife to counter with a direct request like, "I was thinking the kids would really like it if you put them to bed sometimes." Instead when he doesn't volunteer to help with the bedtime routine, Mom feels he doesn't really want to share responsibilities and doesn't care about her. This puzzles him because he is negotiating and wants to do his part.

> **"Men are taught to emphasize negotiation while women are trained in cooperation."**

For men, a good bargaining session is a form of connection. Picture two guys hassling each other in a fun way before agreeing who drives on a fishing trip or picks up beer. They feel like buddies because they are close enough to tease, hassle, and negotiate. A woman, on the other hand, thinks the highest form of love is when a man volunteers to take over some duties. That relieves her and involves him spending more time with their child. If the husband reminds her, she may vaguely remember when teasing, hassling, and negotiating could be fun occasionally. That stuff is not fun now when she is this tired and needs help, *now.*

Women, on the other hand, are trained in cooperation. Women believe, "If I do this for you (and you care about me) you will remember and reciprocate. She expects—but normally doesn't get—the same in return. She will often respond by saying, "Because you don't volunteer more, you don't care." He feels crushed by this criticism since he adores her and the child and doesn't know what she is responding to or talking about because she has not directly asked for anything. He may actually want to be asked and included.

Without conscious effort and understanding of their negotiating styles, and the importance of taking care of both their needs, couples gradually drift into an unequal relationship with a resentful wife and a husband who feels abused by her irritability and anger. Although women joke about men not doing their fair share, women and men don't easily recognize what each partner does to help create and support this situation.

The average woman's mother may not have worked outside the home. Or, her mom may have worked outside the home at a nine-to-five job rather than having a "career" with expectations about travel, speaking engagements or deadlines. If she did work outside the home, she may have done so only after the youngest was in school.

BABY BLUES By Rick Kirkman and Jerry Scott

She also has new burdens her mother didn't. For example, attending every one of your child's games and practices and maybe even coaching or being team mom is a new requirement of parenthood that was not prevalent in the '50s or even the '60s or '70s. (This is a new time-consuming task for some Dads as well.) All these new time commitments, while possibly quite pleasant, add up to less intimate "couple" time together.

Sometimes making roles "equal" becomes a burden. One perceptive and very tired mother of twins explained it to me like this: "Sometimes a completely equal relationship means every little thing has to be decided. I just don't always want to discuss where the mustard should go in the refrigerator or whose turn it is to pick up the kids. My mom just knew her job and did it." Even if she worked harder she didn't waste time negotiating every little thing.

As her comment indicates, happy couples don't necessarily share child care in a rigid, equal way like alternating each diaper change and each meal they prepare. But they do each have a sense of appreciation for what the other brings to the marriage and they communicate that appreciation. They don't keep track of every little thing. Some couples cross train for parenting responsibilities and feel closer. Others divide and conquer the work.

However they manage it, happy couples achieve a balance that works for them. True fairness is flexible and shows a regular and very deep appreciation for the contribution of the other. When couples make conscious decisions as partners about their priorities and the division of labor in the marriage, the process of working together can create a feeling of mutual respect that affects the future happiness of the whole family.

Solving the mundane sleep problems peacefully and resolving marital issues instead of sweeping them under the rug in the race to chase the kids and careers leads to closeness and a deeper friendship between parents. Creating a life together that respects both your wants, wishes, and desires brings you closer and makes you both feel better about yourselves.

SLEEP SOLUTIONS

- If partners don't share a similar vulnerability to sleep deprivation, the two can use their natural inclinations to become a good tag team. The person with more tolerance for sleep disruption handles night duty and naps during the day. The sleep-requiring partner can do the early morning or weekend duty.
- Some couples alternate nights they get up with the baby or one partner takes night duty on weekends while the other partner takes weekdays.
- Dad can bring crying baby to bed so Mom can breast-feed without fully awakening, and Dad can then comfort junior and put him back to bed.
- If both partners have a problem with sleep deprivation, they may need extra help. One exhausted mother of twins hired a baby sitter every day for two hours, hoping to get some housework done. She slept instead and felt guilty, but was less grouchy. This seemed like a good practical solution to me.
- Natural sleep remedies, like valerian root or melatonin work for some people, although others experience significant side effects. Be especially cautious of these solutions if you are breastfeeding!
- Prescription antidepressants such as Zoloft or Prozac can help mitigate the irritability and depression of the sleep disruption for some people. Ironically these both may cause weight gain and further inhibit your already diminished sex drive.
- Anti-anxiety drugs such as Valium and Xanax will give a good night's sleep in the short term, but most are addictive and create insomnia if used repeatedly. They also may dramatically increase any tendency to depression.

If you choose to live better chemically, some careful reading and a good health care professional to help you evaluate the remedies you chose are essential. I cannot list all the side effects here.

Work together making this decision. Often a spouse detects changes in a sleep-deprived or depressed partner's mood sooner and more accurately than the affected person does. If you plan to sleep through the night soundly with medication, be sure your spouse or someone can and will wake up when necessary and that you do not sleep with the baby in your bed. Your solution will be specific to your needs and most successful if you can find one you both support.

Tips for Fostering Fairness and Balance

- **Step in and take the kids.** Send your wife to the bath or out to lunch or let your husband take a nap or watch a game.
- **Switch roles occasionally.** Send your partner on a day or two away if you are the one who always travels.
- **Plan fun time together.** If your partner spends too much time on chores and not enough time having fun, ask how you can help so you plan fun time together. This kind of person needs a plan to feel comfortable having fun. Don't call your partner a stick in the mud.
- **Take the kids** and do something your partner usually does with them. Fix a meal or go to the park.
- **Check in monthly** (put it on the calendar or in your PDA!) with each other about the decisions you've made about the division of the workload and time with your careers versus time for the kids. Are you comfortable with your own decision and with your partner's? Do you have second thoughts? Are your family needs changing in ways that require adjustment?
- **Wash dishes**, empty the dishwasher, or take out the garbage occasionally, even though it isn't your job.
- **Adjust your expectations.** It takes 15 minutes to get kids into the car to go somewhere. The house will be messier than it used to be. Everything—grocery shopping, picking up

clothes at the dry cleaners, and entertaining—will take at least twice as long, sometimes more.

- **Never criticize your partner for a messy house**. Ask what you can do together to turn things around. You can make a new plan to deal with the mess together (although it probably won't work the first time). Joke about the mess together, but don't call your partner a slob or lazy.

- **Clean up a mess.** Partners who work outside the home and don't mind a mess, (and you do) may need a more direct wake-up call. They need to know even if it doesn't matter to them, a clean house matters to you, and if neat matters to one of you, the other will often help. A friend told me that her husband has four areas—his desk, his closet, his sink and the garage—that she doesn't touch and even the housekeeper can't manage. They talked it over and now once a month she says, "It's time—this weekend. I want your areas cleaned up," and he does it!

- **Trade jobs.** Learn how your other half lives. Let the person who balances the checkbook "wrong" or who doesn't clean as well do it exactly that way. It is a brief experiment. Talk about what it feels like.

- **Sit down and make a list of all the household chores,** how often they need to be done, and the hours required. Include time spent on the job making money to pay bills as a chore. Discuss and divide the time in a way that seems equitable so you both get to do what you like most. Decide to skip some stuff or delegate what you don't like. Discuss what you like doing alone and what you really miss doing together.

- **Add up how much relaxed personal time** each of you has whether it's jogging or TV watching. See if you can figure out how to have a bit more personal time without losing couple time.

Work together on your budget, your goals, and your parenting.

6 It Takes a Village to Shelter Your Marriage

We expect that our partner is going to rescue us from the day-to-day rigors of life with kids. The reality is that it takes a village to shelter a healthy marriage.

Parents need to create supportive environments for themselves and their kids and befriend good models to show kids the many ways family members solve problems and enjoy life and each other. Who is going to watch your children so that you can have time alone? Who is going to make you feel safe on your child's first sleep over? Where will you find a sounding board when you doubt your parenting decisions? Who is going to tell you how he or she resolved that perpetual conflict with a spouse?

In some magical places, three and four generations of family members live nearby supporting both children and parents. But for the most part, this is not the case in urban America today. Without a solid support system nearby, many women, especially if they previously enjoyed working outside the home, experience periods of intense loneliness and isolation staying home. However, a supportive village of nice families can help buffer irrational worries and realistic challenges.

Unfortunately, instead of turning to their village or creating a village, the new parents lean too much on each other and wear out the relationship. A new mom often expects her spouse to be her main, and sometimes only, source for warmth and emotional support. Unfortunately, the harried new mom may also begin to see her partner as a quality child care provider who owes her break time from the kids rather than as a romantic partner to take a fun break with.

Meanwhile, the new dad expects the new mom to be as attentive and supportive when he arrives home as she was before the baby. Dad loves his baby but he'd like his wife back the way she was—paying attention to him. Occasionally, couples reverse roles: Dad is the one who is gaga over the new baby and Mom is the one who misses the attention she once had. Each is unaware of how much of a toll the new commitments are taking on their relationship and may blame the other rather than express their sadness about missing time and fun together. These expectations for the partner overburden the marriage.

A strong community of close friends or family is vital to helping with this stress. This network provides both partners with concrete assistance and models for how to deal with new experiences. Having someone to watch your kids can be a vital stress reducer at a critical time. In healthy families, aunts, uncles, reliable young cousins, family friends, and grandparents who adore your children can be trusted caregivers when you need a break. They also can provide invaluable perspective when your child's and/or spouse's unique needs or temperaments are confusing to you.

In the midst of struggling with parenting and marital issues, my clients often ask in a desperate tone, "Is this normal?!?" Family and friends help you gain perspective on the wide variety of temperaments, conflicts, and issues that are normal. An understanding mother-in-law can help explain how she came to terms with a night-owl husband. A good friend can let you know how they coped with a partner who simply doesn't believe in recording checks until the bank calls with an overdraft notice. My sister now chuckles about how her son sweated through his first years because the books said to dress your child as warmly as you dress yourself, but he had his daddy's warmer metabolism. It wasn't until a more experienced mom pointed out the baby was sweating. Oops! When you live many miles from family and friends, it is important to create your own family of choice nearby. Special needs children require a special village. If you have a "special needs" child, your own relatives may not understand the nuances of caring for him or her. It may be harder to build your own couple network when you have a special needs child, as well. New parents can be pretty judgmental and skittish. But someone, somewhere outside of your family has successfully raised a child or children very much like yours. They are in your community or can be found through the Internet. With the support and resources of this community, it will be possible to find the time and energy, so you and your partner can support each other and your child.

> **Parents often ask in a desperate tone, "Is this normal?!?"**

For people whose parents and grandparents are substance abusers, verbal abusers, or otherwise unsuitable, it becomes even more critical to develop a family of choice. Even if a partner has one good parent, he or she may have not seen a model for how a good marriage works.

Often people from emotionally abusive family situations have a hard time seeing that relationships with helpful people in the community are possible. They also may not know how to establish a family of choice or they may be afraid of being rejected if they try. If you feel completely alone in your community, seek help from your church or a professional to find the support you need.

As you're developing your village, most people notice that their friendships change in several ways after the birth of their first child. Women experience more disruption in their social world after the arrival of kids than at any other time in their lives—and more so than men. If a mom knows what to expect and can talk with old friends as the changes occur, she can deepen these friendships and escape the feelings of guilt or craziness as her relationships evolve. Mom may even be able to maintain relationships with childless friends that she might otherwise have lost. She also won't wear herself out trying to meet their or her own expectations that no longer fit her new life.

Girlfriends without children have strong social expectations such as spending time together in adult conversation, exchanging gifts, talking on the phone, and attending each other's events. A mother who routinely juggles multiple kids' birthday parties is less enamored of exchanging gifts. And, she definitely has a harder time talking on the phone now that her children demand and need her attention. Even within extended families, frustrations can arise between grown siblings who have children and those who don't.

My very patient youngest sister, who had children before I did, struggled through buying birthday and holiday gifts for each of the twenty people in our extended family. As time passed and I had my own kids, I began to realize why she had been gently suggesting for years that we no longer needed to exchange so many gifts. After a few Christmases with my own kids, I eagerly agreed to draw names for presents so that each person had to buy only one gift. Soon we agreed to buy gifts only for those under thirteen.

Particularly if they used to work, new moms report loneliness as their number-one complaint, possibly due to their isolation.

Friends with kids, on the other hand, understand problems with time constraints and the art of making conversation between interruptions by little ones. Friends without kids may grow quickly impatient or judgmental about how mom has "let" the children interfere. Even when relationships with childless friends don't end, some alterations in a couple's social life are inevitable. While changing or ending these relationships can be sad, it opens the door to new ones with people who will support you raising your kids.

Shortly after the birth of my first child, my friend, Judy, startled me by saying how lonely she felt after the birth of her first child. Judy always seemed so outgoing and has always had a large circle of friends. What startled me was that I felt lonely, too. I soon learned that many new moms feel this way. A very happily married woman told me she felt so lonely for adult companionship when her kids were small that she would long to go to her husband's work dinners, which she previously avoided like the plague. My sister confessed that she cross-country skied in the middle of a Vermont snowstorm with her baby on her back to make a planned mom's meeting just to get out of the house!

Particularly if they used to work, new moms report loneliness as their number-one complaint, possibly due to their isolation. Studies show that the risk for depression is highest in this period of a woman's life. If the new mom becomes mildly depressed, she may become even more removed from both her partner and her friends. As she withdraws, the new father may feel isolated, as well. Because she is less inclined to leave the house, Dad may feel isolated from their social life.

A mom's isolation is softened if she is part of a close-knit community of friends who are having children at about the same time. The feeling may also be less intense with the birth of a second or third child because the mom now has an active, talkative child already at home, has more girlfriends with children, and has resolved loneliness issues with her spouse. On the other hand, the second-time mom may be so busy meeting the needs of two children that she may become lonelier because she has less time for her friends and her spouse.

Not too surprisingly, many men also feel this loneliness, though they rarely say so because "loneliness" isn't a macho word. Yet they feel cut off because the new mom is freshly enamored with the new baby. Many men will say they feel abandoned or that they miss the romance. They, in turn, may blame the new mom.

Most couples feel a sense of loneliness because the structure of their relationship shifts so profoundly. It helps to talk about that shift and accept that one or both of you may be less than ecstatically happy about aspects of the new baby experience. As a couple and as individuals, both partners will need to resolve how to handle feelings of loneliness and the abrupt change of identity from adult to Mom or Dad.

BABY BLUES By Rick Kirkman and Jerry Scott

Comedian Rob Becker, in his performance called "Defending the Caveman," suggests that men speak only 2,000 words a day and women speak 7,000! And by the time they get home, men have used up all 2,000. To a bored and lonely new mom at home all day with a demanding but non-"adult" speaking infant, this is frustrating. She's ready to talk, but he has little to talk about. What a new mom really needs is time with other moms so that when she is with Dad she can concentrate on their mutual interests other than the children. If she gets this friend time, she will be a more interesting and happier partner.

Unfortunately, sometimes neither partner understands these changing needs for social contact and both feel adrift. Both need to recognize the importance to their couple relationship of balancing Mom's increased desire to get out and connect with other people. Rather than support her, too often a new dad feels more neglected and/or threatened that she needs time with parents other than him. When both partners understand the balance problem is normal, they can more easily resolve it.

Finally, another relationship challenge is likely to occur if she rejoins the workforce, as many women do sometime before their child turns six. Suddenly, rather than needing to get out, she wants to be home. Meanwhile, if Dad's daily routine remains relatively stable, he may find the sudden shifts in Mom's social needs confusing and uncomfortable, even a little "crazy." If the new mom looks to the new dad to respond and fill all of these rapidly shifting social needs, he is bound to fall short. Both can be frustrated. He is also likely to try to enforce an old solution like: "Let's just go away for the weekend and do the things we used to do." But the new mom (and sometimes the new dad) may have a hard time separating from the child to carry out that solution because separation doesn't feel right just then.

Although new dads don't usually notice that they need new friends, couples are generally happier when Dad gets to know other dads with kids of or near the same age. Socializing occasionally with other contented couples with kids serves as a kind of marriage insurance. Other couples will have similar issues and complaints. It is reassuring to vent and sometimes learn creative ideas to resolve normal kid problems.

While new parents need the support of a village, they also need to avoid being overwhelmed by it. Gracefully setting clear boundaries for your village is an important skill. When couples first get married, they often need to resolve the issue of how much time they are going to spend socially with friends and family. When a new baby arrives, this issue has to be revisited and resolved again. For example, right after the baby is born, family and friends may suddenly start drop-in visits when Mom has the least energy to handle them (after all, you are always home now). Along with these visits, advice and family folklore may come raining down, inundating both Mom and Dad.

BABY BLUES

Although a very small number of women experience full depression during pregnancy, studies published by the American Psychological Association suggest that 50 to 80 percent of women experience "baby blues," a mild postpartum drop in mood. This occurs about the third or fourth day after delivery and lasts from one to 14 days. Postpartum depression, on the other hand, is much more serious and occurs for some women from six weeks to four months after delivery and may last six months to a year. About 16 percent of women experience this more serious problem.

Depression occurs most frequently among women who have marital difficulties, had depression during the pregnancy, and/or experienced significant anxiety and life stress before the birth of the baby. Thus, in one of those tricky circles of life, sometimes depression is caused by marital difficulties, and sometimes, marital difficulties may result from a biologically based depression. This circular relationship can spiral up or down, depending on whether the marriage relationship aggravates the depression or supports the person through the depression.

If you are depressed, a professional can help you and your partner eliminate the depression and save your marriage. If both of you aren't at least a little more hopeful and a little less depressed after four weeks of therapy, find a new professional. Depression is a serious threat to your marriage, but once identified, it is usually readily treated.

It really helps when a new mom and dad support each other in making sure they are comfortable with village members. You will feel closer when you make decisions together about when to include others. Many a new mom and dad have to learn how to uninvite members of the village as well as include them.

Setting limits and building your village or community together can help you both know that your feelings and values as a couple come first. Otherwise, the cocoon will be invaded. The sense of family can be weakened. The warm feeling that you know each other intimately and can play and have fun together can get diluted. Then you may begin to feel like strangers. The sense that you are a couple, a special team, will be enhanced if you share relaxed alone time together as well as good fun with great friends at other times. Some couples set up a socializing schedule or calendar to make sure their own personal time, couple time, "just our little family time" and extended family times don't get lost in a too-busy village.

A good village supports your values so your kids accept your expectations and rules more easily. As kids grow, adult friends with children reassure one another that the multiple crises of parenting are normal. Later, you can keep watch over each other's kids as they gain independence. Friends also help parents broaden their horizons. Interacting with a strong village of other families, parents and kids learn the different ways that people celebrate holidays, manage money, and relate to each other. Most importantly for the marriage, a network of happily married couples gives you healthy models for strong relationships and, if they also offer shared childcare, they give you some couple time together to enjoy your marriage. A good village supports a new little family.

Creating Your Family Village

Few families are lucky enough to have all these roles filled by relatives and friends already in their lives. You can add village members of choice to fill in gaps. Whether you pay them for childcare, exchange babysitting, or they volunteer, find people who share your values. Religious groups traditionally can be a good place to find community support. If you are not religious, participating in local school and community activities can provide a chance to meet people who are child friendly. Good support will feel good and enhance your marriage.

Don't expect to find these people all at once. These special people sometimes arrive in your life just when you need them. I am so grateful for people who have filled these roles in our lives. Here are some types of people to watch for when creating your village.

Old Souls: Wise grandmothers and grandfathers, widowed or not, who have or had a happy marriage are great. Though they may not be your kids' grandparents, they have solved the problem of staying together 25 years or more and raised caring competent kids in reasonable financial stability. It is best if they live nearby and feel lucky to have time to spend with your kids, maybe even when the kids are sick. Although some young moms find old souls intimidating and overly helpful, older women or couples can be the best babysitters.

"Older Siblings" to the Parents: Couple friends who are happily married and have a child one to four years older than your oldest can give you a heads up about what's coming in school and what is ahead developmentally for your child (and your marriage).

Aunts and Uncles to the Kids: Responsible young adult figures who find your kids adorable and have lots of energy are a real blessing. This allows kids to have one-on-one uninterrupted time with an adult. Sometimes aunts or friends who have only girls adopt boys or vice versa so they can enjoy a different energy.

Godparents: Two people who support your values who can step in to raise your children if you were disabled or ill can also spend special time with your kids. Traditionally, they attended your wedding and also oversaw your child's religious education. (My kids say it helps if they are rich and shower your kids with wonderful presents.)

Cousins: Both older and younger kids who are being raised in homes that support your values can help your children learn to get along with kids at different developmental stages. Older children of close friends, teenage coaches, tutors, or baby-sitters can be great role models.

Nearby Family Friends and Neighbors: People who have kids about the same ages as yours are great for sharing a carpool or picking up the kids when your car breaks down.

Mates: *Most happily married couples have happily married friends.* Whether you choose to work out of the home, in the home, or be Mr. Mom, friends who have made the same choice help your sanity. If your friends are competent, functioning adults with nice children and loving marriages, they can provide valuable perspective for those rough moments in your marriage. Besides, they are fun.

Friends and family overlap in various roles, but they can form a magical safety net to support you, your family and your marriage. The neat thing about a family of choice—unlike your relatives, who can be a mixed bag—is that you choose them.

Tips for Creating an Intimate Friendship Circle

- **Set a routine** that gets Mom out of the house every day if she is home full time. Take a walk or trip to the park. Go to the library for the weekly book reading. Mom will meet other mothers, and these activities are healthy and stimulate the child as well.
- **Join a church or religious group** or a Mommy-and-Me group. Invite people to your house afterwards.
- **Plan a family camping trip** or short vacation with another family.
- **Start a monthly book club** of mothers and dads and take your kids. It is chaotic at first, but people say it works because the book is a shared experience.
- **Get a walking partner/exercise partner** for regular walks, with or without the kids.

- **Make park dates or play dates** and let the dads take the kids occasionally.
- **Check your social calendar.** Your list of obligatory social engagements without the kids may need to shrink to allow time for yourselves and for the new little person in your schedule.
- **Calendar fun.** One couple does Calendar Night about once a month or so and looks at their weekend and vacation plans several months ahead. They plan who they want to spend time with instead of making passive choices as they respond to invitations.
- **Make Granny nanny time.** If you are lucky enough to have a grandparent or friend who wants to be close to your child, set up a time for them to take the baby for a yogurt or a regular trip to the park. Then have a date with your spouse. This works best if you start when the child is very small and keep the outings brief to avoid grandparent shock and child meltdowns. Gradually extend the time so they get used to having a special time with Granddad or Aunt Suzy. Be sure to express your gratitude to them.
- **Find babysitters for dates.** If you don't have a willing grandparent (and even if you do), scout out an experienced childcare person who will be available to babysit for your "parent alone" time and for emergencies. Grandma may leave town to be with her dying sister for six weeks, or go on a trip to the Caribbean with a new boyfriend. Some grandmas have more exciting lives than we do right now.
- **Consider an online support group** of other parents to share ideas, especially if your child has special needs.
- **Find neighborhood help.** Likewise, as your kids get older, hire the nice neighborhood kids you admire to help around the house. They will work for almost nothing and they will be great babysitters in a few years. Your kids will love them and may even copy some good habits along the way. You will have more time for your relationship.

- **Find a compatible friend for exchanging childcare.** Another mother with kids can help for visits to the doctor
- when you don't want to take all the kids or to arrange trades for date nights.
- **Take time to talk about your village.** Discuss whether the village is feeling like a support or a drain on you and your marriage. Take action together to keep it in balance.
- **Thank helpful people** in your village warmly and often.

7 Chance for a New Start

New parents think that babies are a chance for a new start. A new baby is like New Year's Day for some people. They start making resolutions. "I'll never say, 'Because I said so!' 'I won't lose my temper,' and 'I'm not going to shout at my husband, especially in front of the kids,'" are some common resolutions.

What most well-intentioned couples fail to factor in is that their own parents provided a potent learning experience for them. Even though you swear you will be different from your parents, when you least expect it, you will open your mouth and your parents' words will jump out. Unless your parents were blissfully happy while you were growing up, those things that pop out aren't always good for your marriage or your kids.

In a crisis, we often do what we have seen done and not what we have planned. For example, an average person, untrained as a lifeguard, who sees someone drowning will often just react by jumping into the icy waters and drowning with the victim. A lifeguard is trained to throw the life ring or extend a pole first, saving the victim and protecting his own life as well. But it takes practice to learn that. The stress of raising kids makes all parents the untrained lifeguards of our children and especially our marriage. In moments of stress, we may do what we saw done most, like saying "because I said so" or not saving time for the marriage. These reactions can be good or bad depending on our own experiences. Kids bring out the best and the worst in us. And if you were in an unhappy marriage, as I said before, the earlier marriage may also influence you in surprising, often negative ways.

Remember that just as your parents influenced you, your in-laws influenced your partner. By watching your in-laws, you may have some warning about the ghostlike behaviors that may be appearing in your marriage. Instead of critically judging what you see, think about what positive outcome the behavior has for them. Perhaps your father-in-law acting jealous makes your mother-in-law feel cared about. Maybe instead of making your mother-in-law feel neglected, your father-in-law's fishing trips are a substitute for fighting and give each of them a breather. Ask your village members how they handle behavior that you anticipate will make you feel upset. By being gently curious about what works for them and why, rather than judgmental, you can work together with your partner to develop comfortable routines that work for you.

Instead, unfortunately, in-laws can become the focus of frustration and anger in many marriages. Focusing on changing yourself and on how to work with your partner is better than trying to "fix" your partner or your in-laws. For example, you might start to understand your partner's habit of interrupting constantly when you watch your in-laws fight for airtime at family gatherings. Then, you might start to learn how to deflect the interruptions or accept them. Or by observing and being curious about your in-laws highly conflicted but long-lasting marriage, you may begin to understand your partner's need to avoid conflict. Furthermore, you might concentrate on how to draw out your partner's view of an issue, instead of insisting yours be heard first.

BET 5:1 ON LASTING LOVE

The most fascinating finding from long-term research in John Gottman's Seattle Love Lab was that these happy couples, even when arguing about a major issue, had a five-to-one ratio of positive to negative words gestures. When each partner expresses five times as much appreciation as negativity, starts discussions gently, makes requests politely, and consistently looks for and perceives the partner's good intentions, your marriage will work 90-plus percent of the time. I have seen people turn bad marriages to good ones in 30 days when they adjust their attitude and express gratitude, touch and appreciation first, and five times more often than negatives. To jump-start their marriages, they set a goal of no criticism for 30 days. This is a true new start.

Unfortunately, 99.9 percent of people focus on changing their partner. But if we concentrate, we can change the things about ourselves we want to change. Here's how: Write down three unproductive, embarrassing or annoying things that your own parents do with each other that make you uncomfortable. Then write down three things that you wish they'd do instead. Tape those three positive things to your mirror to remind yourself to do them. Most people have trouble coming up with the three positives. It's not cheating to ask another happily married person what they might do in a difficult situation.

Behaviors That Don't Work (and sample fixes)

- **Instead of expecting your partner to mind read,** it is better to tell your partner how you feel, without using the word "you." A poor example is: "*You* make me so pissed off because *you* are so: stupid, lazy...." (Fill in the negative words.) Better would be: "It scares me when you do that. It frustrates me when you do that." Or even better, leave out the negative description and say, "I feel close to you when you help me clean up after dinner.... (or whatever you want to have happen next time)."
- **Instead of withdrawing,** a better step would be to warn your partner that you need time to reflect about this issue, say you would like to give it some serious thought, and then talk about it at a specific time like after the kids are in bed or the next morning. During the break, try to reflect on looking at

your contribution to the conflict first before blaming your partner.

- **Try to look at your contribution first** when you are thinking it over. *Then* try to understand *your partner's* behavior. Ask yourself what your partner was trying to accomplish or what the goal was when they did or said what they did. Do **not** ask "Why" questions in exasperation, like, *"Why did you ever..."* or *"Why don't you ever..."* or *"Why do you always have to...!!??"* Assume good intentions on your partner's part. Do not create more shame. Your partner may now regret or be embarrassed about what happened. Highlight whatever shared goals you have in the future. Instead of "What were you trying to accomplish?" ask this: "How could we work better in the future?"

- **For those of you who refuse to compromise,** get over yourself or you are going to be lonely. Seriously, try to think of three other things that you have compromised about in the recent past, before you refuse to compromise on this. If you cannot remember compromising, ask yourself why it is important that you win on everything. *While you're at it, ask yourself if your need to win is more important than saving your marriage.*

- **Always acting like the victim and feeling abused** is another pitfall in a marriage. If this is your problem, get help learning to anticipate how to respond when you feel your partner is pushing your boundaries. If you have trouble setting boundaries like, "I'm uncomfortable with this plan," practice how you can kindly and calmly set boundaries, *before* you get upset.

- **If you have a problem with drinking** too much, seek out AA or professional help. Help is also in order if you find yourself threatening violence or always caving in because you feel threatened. If your partner won't go to counseling, go by yourself.

Unfortunately people sometimes have such severe traumas in their past, like sexual molestation, severe verbal or physical abuse, or alcoholic parents, that being in any close intimate parenting/partnering relationship is very uncomfortable. Though they love their partners, they have trouble with sex or intimacy. Fortunately, an accelerated information processing method discovered by Francine Shapiro called Eye Movement Desensitization and Reprocessing (EMDR) allows people to resolve these issues fairly rapidly and couples to feel much closer and more comfortable together.

The good news is that no matter how bad you think your past is, you can have a good relationship if you work on it with your partner. In fact, some of my couples with the most painful and abusive pasts develop the best, most intimate relationships working together in therapy. They feel a genuine and profound gratitude and say things like, "My own family was such a mess, that what we have feels like heaven. It surprises me every day." Over time, learning to deal with and resolve the issues from your past can lead to genuine sharing and a sense of comfort and solace that feels miraculous. Such work and understanding leads to a sense of equality. Each partner feels equally valued, equally important, and equally respected.

THE SHORT LIST
THINGS THAT DON'T WORK FOR HAPPY MARRIAGE
(and Sample Fixes)

Expecting your partner to know what you are feeling.
Tell them how you feel.

Expecting your partner to know what you like and dislike.
Tell them what you want/expect calmly before the situation occurs.

Expecting help without asking for it.
Ask for help as politely as if you were asking a stranger.

Criticizing or ridiculing a spouse for their taste, preferences or behavior.
Act the way you would like your children to treat a visiting aunt.

Withdrawing into silence when conflict comes up.
Warn your partner you need quiet time to reflect on this and that you will come back to talk about it at a specific time.

Keeping track of mistakes.
Remind your partner of something they do well when they goof. Better yet, remind them of your last blooper.

Blaming the partner.
Look at your contribution first. Then try to understand their behavior and why it may have occurred. Assume good intentions on their part. They may now regret or be embarrassed about what they did.

Yelling to make someone listen.
Be curious why they didn't hear you the first time. "This is the third time you asked me to tell you when we are going to the Joneses. Are you unhappy about going?" "This is the second time I asked you to fix the sink and you agreed. Is there a problem getting in the way?"

Keeping score of who does what.
Strive to always do 60 percent of the load and ask for help when you need it before you get hostile.

Saying "I told you so."
Don't. (If you can't help yourself, ask if they are surprised that you were right.)

Never saying what you want for presents.
Act delighted with what you get or get over it and make a wish list for your partner to choose from next time.

Never saying what you want to do for fun.
Have fun no matter what your partner chooses or make a suggestion. Some couples have the "reluctant spouse plan," a quarterly couple getaway to get them used to making the plan.

Tips for Handling Ghosts from the Past

- **Always work on your own ghosts first.** If you must analyze, analyze yourself first. Ask yourself why your partner's behavior bothers you so much. Answer the question with an "I" statement not a "he" statement. For example, "When he comes home and watches TV instead of offering to help, it reminds me of my mother and dad and I feel angry," not "When he comes home and reads he is sooo selfish and inconsiderate." Dig deeper and figure out what ghosts in your past are stirring. Then work on how you can change, like learning to ask cheerfully and directly for help. We will talk about the blame game later, a ghost that is often handed down from generation to generation. (If it is a big problem, like domestic violence, substance abuse, or infidelity, get time away and get help for yourself first so you can make good decisions. It is not your fault, and no one thinks well under stress.)
- **Ask yourself** if there is something that you do that encourages your partner's undesired behavior. Consider asking your spouse or a friend the same question.
- **If your partner is giving you the silent treatment:** Say something like, "I notice you don't want to talk to me. Is there something you are upset about?" Or, "Did something I said/did upset you? Are you angry with me? Perhaps I

haven't been a very good listener, and when you've tried to talk I've bossed you around or taken over the conversation? I am really sad to realize I have probably been doing this to you."

- **If your partner criticizes you,** turn the criticizing on its head with *positive reframing.* For example, if your partner says you are a control freak, instead of going nuts about his behavior respond with something like "You're right, I may have a tendency to be over controlling," and use it to open a discussion: "We seem to be having a conflict right now but as bad as that feels, I am thinking it may be a way to figure out how to get closer and handle this differently in the future."

- **Before you request a big change** from your spouse, get an independent opinion from a happily married person you trust, who knows and likes your spouse.

- **If you would like your partner to change something,** do not describe what you hate.

- **Ask for what you would like to see** instead, and tell him/her why and how good it would make you feel. Then reward your partner enthusiastically when he/she does it.

- **Write your change request down and read it carefully before you give it to your partner.** How would you feel if you were receiving it? Are you asking your partner to do something or not do something? Asking for something positive works better than asking to eliminate something.

- **Never talk badly about your in-laws.** If you need to sort out your feelings about your in-laws, talk to a friend or a counselor who will never talk to your spouse or your in-laws about your concerns. This is true even if your partner complains about his or her parents or siblings a lot. Remember this simple rule: I can criticize my family, but not my partner's family and vice versa.

- **Listen sympathetically or be gently curious** when your partner complains about his or her family. Ask him how it makes him feel. Avoid joining in enthusiastically with the complaints. This increases negativity and doesn't help either of you move on.

- **Be curious rather than critical** about why your in-laws do something unusual. Encourage them to tell you stories about their past and their relationship. They have ghosts too. Things that seem strange at first will seem less mysterious. Your interest will make you more popular.
- **If your in-laws do something that really makes you crazy,** tell your spouse that his or her parents' behavior makes you uncomfortable, doesn't work for you, or hurts your feelings. Do not expect your spouse to understand why it makes you uncomfortable, although she/he may understand perfectly. Just ask for what you would like instead. Be careful. Make sure that it is something you really need. Don't put everything on the list.
- **If you are both at a loss about how to manage your in-laws better,** ask an objective outsider in your village for suggestions.
- **Do not criticize or compare your spouse or children to your in-laws** except on things that show them in a favorable light.
- **Think of things that you genuinely admire about each of your in-laws** and relatives. Be specific and genuine. Have a goal of five things. My favorite line was, "My husband has a wonderful family. No one gets drunk or fights at family gatherings, and they like kids."
- **Be ready to mention your five positive things** before you suggest changes in the way you as a couple deal with the relatives. Easier still, choose to marry someone whose family is great.
- **Set goals for your parenting together,** not achievement goals to pressure your kids.
- **Set people-skills goals together** with your spouse for your own family. Practicing social skills—like making positive requests of your kids—will polish your skills and your partner's skills with each other. Teaching your kids will help

you change habits. Working together makes being married fun, and you are less likely to do automatic things from the past.

- **Set goals for your marriage together.** Revise them regularly. Planning and talking about what you want rather than what you are unhappy about creates a positive atmosphere where good habits develop.

Summary of Part 1

As you can see from the last seven chapters, equality, sharing, support, and cocooning are *not* normal predictable consequences of having a baby. Some couples achieve these ideals, but most do not. Once a baby arrives, partners go through rapid changes in their relationship, but often mom and dad move in different directions. These changes happen while the couple is excited, sleep deprived, exhausted and overwhelmed. They have little time to reflect on what is happening. As the pace quickens, these changes snowball. Home life, social life, sex life, and living environments change dramatically. Mom may stop her career. Dad may intensify his. The division of labor in the house shifts. By the time the child is three or four, the parents' relationship may have become something neither wanted nor expected. If a second child arrives, their couple relationship may go on permanent hold or be lost. If the issues go unresolved too long, efforts to salvage the marriage or create the marriage that you both dreamed of creating together come too late.

On the other hand, creating a few good habits that support your relationship can dramatically improve your marriage in a very short time. I have seen a marriage turn around when the husband called to make a first therapy appointment on the way to the divorce settlement conference. Usually things don't change that late, but this man was very motivated. A sincere desire to change can produce dramatic results.

No matter how bad your past is, you can have a good relationship if you work on it together. In fact, some of my couples with the most painful and abusive pasts develop the best relationships working together in therapy. They feel a genuine and profound gratitude for what they have created in their own marriage in contrast to the serious problems of their own childhood and parents. They become even more deeply committed to each other and grateful for their time together than couples without such scary, problematic pasts.

Over time, good habits can lead to genuine sharing, a sense of comfort and solace that feels miraculous. Such work and understanding leads to a sense of equality. Each partner feels equally valued, equally important, and equally respected. Working together makes it possible.

These equally valued partners in happy, thriving couples divide the responsibilities of marriage in many different ways. There are no cookie-cutter solutions. Certain general rules are the same in happy marriages. In thriving marriages:

- Both partners make time for each other alone without kids.
- Each feels they can get their partner's attention easily when needed.
- Both know they come first with their partner.
- Both can share their feelings and know they will be heard.
- Neither feels lonely or shut out.
- Both feel if they need contact, connection, or comfort their partner will be there.
- Each can lean on the other when anxious or unsure.
- Even when they fight or disagree, they feel sure they will find a way to come together and work it out.
- Both feel if they need reassurance about how important they are to their partner, they can get it.
- Both feel they can confide almost anything to each other.
- Both know the other cares about their hurts, joys, and fears.
- Even when they are apart, both feel connected to each other.
- Both are comfortable and committed to spending at least 20 minutes a day communicating eyeball to eyeball, email to email, phone to phone or some combination of these.

- Both partners express appreciation and fondness frequently in ways their partner recognizes.
- Both partners really get to know their partner's friends, interests, aspirations, and worries.
- Both partners actively contribute to the marriage. Neither feels put upon or used.
- Both partners have a good time doing little things together.
- Both partners express genuine appreciation for what the other contributes.
- Both partners influence each other.
- Both feel comfortable working together to solve problems.
- Both can talk about problems without blame.
- Both expect to put in more than 50 percent of the work. Some contribute in similar ways as when both work outside the home, trade meals and laundry, and spend similar amounts of time with the baby. Others take very different roles. Whether their contributions are similar or different, both feel that each contributes either monetarily or by household chores or childcare. Each feels they contribute what is right for them.
- Both sense that the division of labor is fair, if not precisely equal. They come up with a plan, however loosely patched together, that works for them so that they are not constantly upset when their expectations are not met.
- Both have a shared vision of their marriage and what is important to them.
- Most importantly, both feel they can be comfortable and close, trusting their partner.

Expectations are critical. Quietly unhappy, resigned couples know what they expect and are chronically disappointed. Eventually the couple comes to a resolution that doesn't work well for either spouse. They don't feel close. But at least the relationship is predictable and keeps a kind of peace, so that they are not constantly upset. The marriage functions but neither partner is very happy.

Happy couples, on the other hand, work together to understand each other's expectations. Each partner has adjusted his or her own expectations to fit their spouse's contribution. Both have adjusted their expectations to fit the reality of children. Together they have created a uniquely satisfying relationship. Happy couples work harder to have more.

Part Two

Normal Marriages—
Real Problems

8 Who Is This Person I Married?

As I work with young couples, I try to give them a sense of the developmental stages. My thoughts on these stages are adapted from the excellent book *In Quest of a Mythical Mate* by a long-married therapist couple, Ellyn Bader and Pete Pearson. Pete's blog is wonderful. I often forward it to clients.

Stage 1 is what I call the **Bliss Stage.** You and your partner feel that you are made for each other, and no matter how different your backgrounds are, you bask in the things that you both like. You seem destined to be together because you like the same music and movies, you may share the same religious beliefs, you like the same car or truck and, more importantly, you enjoy a powerful sexual attraction.

In the Bliss Stage, couples count all the ways they are perfectly matched and simply ignore the ways that they don't quite see eye to eye. Sometimes the biggest attraction is that the other person seems to genuinely like you just the way you are. This feeling of oneness and belonging together is the underlying and important foundation that supports a marriage through tough times.

Stage 2: The arrival of kids often leads couples out of the blissful stage to Stage 2. In this stage, the **Differences Stage,** we begin to distance a bit from our partner and think to ourselves, "Who *is* this person I married and why did I choose him or her to be the parent of my child?" Sometimes it is more like "Who the heck have I married?" Each partner begins to notice annoying differences—lots of them. They also begin to realize that some differences are not likely to be resolved without compromise or just plain acceptance. And that compromise means that they will be giving up something even if it is a fantasy of what your

ge would be. Without some perspective it can feel like a
icant loss, like you are giving up some part of yourself
forever—not a comfortable feeling. Although this often feels
devastating and deeply sad, moving on is not only healthy but
necessary to survive this stage and develop a stronger, more
rewarding relationship.

Although couples with or without children naturally move
on to the second stage, it is unfortunate that the beginning of this
difficult second stage often coincides with the arrival of the first
child. People who avoid resolving this crisis by withdrawing or
avoiding each other, or fighting bitterly and playing the blame
game, do not discuss their compromises. Instead of working
through this stage, they do not grieve their lost fantasies and
create a new life. They often feel lonely and may spend years cut
off from their spouses, and then get a divorce when the kids are
grown.

Having children often moves us prematurely into this
stage because we come face to face with what we want for
ourselves and our children and whether we are living in a way we
want our kids to emulate. Children reveal our values for us. Many
little compromises we accepted as okay for just the two of us
don't seem okay for our kids.

People react to this stage in a number of ways.

People react to this stage in a number of ways depending
on their personal style. Often they feel heartbroken and
disappointed that the marriage isn't turning out the way they
pictured. They are frustrated. In this period, each person may
fantasize about the end of the marriage. I have had more than one
woman tell me that she has had visions of her partner being hit by
a truck! Those who don't dream about the end of the marriage
may still deeply grieve for the marriage that might have been.
Some people spend many sad, frustrating years trying to get their
partner to change so they can live out their fantasy.

The Five Stages of Couples

Stage 5 Bonded: Mutual Respect and Affection
We share a strong bond *and* admire each other as individuals.

Stage 4: Friends Again

Stage 3: I am me!
Separate Identities

Stage 2: Who are you? Discovery of Differences

Stage 1 Bliss: We are One; Made For Each Other

Stage 2 is the stage when people decide to get a divorce, even if they linger in Stage 2 for ten or even 17 years (yes, 17 or even 20 years—until the child graduates), not resolving anything and trying to find the courage to take the final step of divorce. Faced with the hard work of compromise and of reconciling differences, many people opt out of their marriage, either by starting an affair or by just becoming emotionally distant. Learning to accept someone as they really are and to accept their needs for intimacy and closeness requires looking at oneself and letting go of the fantasy of what your partner might have become. This is even harder for some. This is the stage during which an affair is most likely.

Couples in this second stage are at even greater risk for affairs when one partner travels a lot or when the family has moved and now lives a long distance from their familiar village of family and friends. Affairs are particularly appealing because they are usually conducted in a private, adults-only environment where talking in whole sentences, listening attentively, and dressing attractively are encouraged.

If step-kids are involved, this stage is even more intense. Both parents may harbor a strong romantic fantasy that *this* time they will get the marriage right. Unfortunately, opportunities for conflict multiply with one or two previous "nightmare" marriages in the mix and older children who have very different expectations. Jealousies about who spends time with whom and when are piled on top of the typical differences a couple may have in their backgrounds.

If your problem seems impossible and entrenched, seek counseling. Most people who seek counseling at this stage try to seduce the therapist to fix the other person. However, a good therapist will help them move on to the next stage by teaching them to focus on their own emotions, wants, needs, and desires. A good therapist will teach them each how to kindly and effectively ask for and give support. Looking at your own wants, needs, and desires rather than arguing what is the 'right" and "wrong" way to do things moves each person to Stage 3.

The Blame Game*

	Blaming the Other	Blaming Yourself	Taking Responsibility
What you tell yourself	"What a JERK!" "She has no right to feel this way!" "It is all his fault." "Everyone would agree that is colossally stupid!"	"It's all my fault." "This is hopeless. I give up." "Nothing I ever do works." "I am a failure."	"I'll try to understand the mistakes I've made so I can learn from them." "I apologize." "I talk about how to make restitution and/or do it better next time."
How you feel	Angry, resentful, hurt, irritated, frustrated	Guilty, ashamed, inferior, anxious, hopeless	Conscientious, curious (mixed with healthy sadness and apprehension) concern and, if appropriate, remorseful
How you communicate	You argue, insisting he or she is wrong, possibly bringing in lots of negative past events.	You withdraw and refuse to engage your partner or cry and tearfully repeat what you failed at	You listen and try to find some truth in your partners' point of view or at least how they experience something differently than you do.
What this leads to	Endless fighting, bitterness, angry explosions.	Isolation, depression, loneliness	Resolution of conflict, greater intimacy, trust, satisfaction

*Adapted from: *Feeling Good Together: the Secret to Making Troubled Marriages Work*, By David D. Burns, 2008. Published by Broadway Books, a division of Random House, Inc.

Stage 3, the Identity Stage, is the **"Who am I?"** stage. In Stage 3, you decide to make your marriage work or not to have an affair, or you have ended an affair and then stepped back and asked yourself what is really important to you. This is when you look at the conflicts and disagreements between the two of you to decide what kind of partner you want to be, not to catalogue the failings of your partner. This stage is critical for yourself, your relationship, and the development of your family. Although self-examination is difficult and to some it seems to be a lifelong pursuit, most people move through it in a year or two, maybe four at the most. Then again, some people get lost in this stage if they focus solely on their own self-development and cannot address how their independent self fits into a relationship or a family.

In this stage, you develop an awareness of how each person in the family has separate and very different goals, needs, and desires. Strong families focus on how each person will get their needs and goals met and how the family can, at the same time, shelter and support individuals. As you become better at understanding that each of you has different needs and each of you needs support, you begin to choose your battles carefully and your accommodations thoughtfully. Compromises can be seen as a gift to your partner and your marriage rather than a request to change your core personality.

You ask yourself, "Can I begin to change myself and my attitudes if it means peace in the house?" You consider what kinds of activities get you into a calm, patient, or self-reflective mode. You ask yourself, "Is there something personal like gym time or writing time or going back to school that I put on hold for the kids and the relationship that would not only make me a better person, but also a better, less irritable partner? What helps me to be a sane and safe (non-hostile) companion?" You may need counseling by yourself rather than as a couple at this point to sort things out. You may learn what you are doing, thinking, or feeling that gets in the way of compromise.

Strong families focus on how each person will get their needs and goals met and how the family can, at the same time, shelter and support individuals.

However, if your marriage has serious problems, you may address the issue of whether you and the kids are better off in the marriage or out of the marriage. Sometimes the situation is critical—like violence or chronic substance abuse—and you may choose to divorce because the differences are too harmful to your children or yourself. If your marriage is relatively sound, you begin to address how two people with very separate identities can live comfortably in the same relationship.

Stage 4, the Friends Again Stage, is when couples decide to be friends. Many couples tell me that they just *decide* to stop fighting and to be civil, although they may still feel a bit distant and mistrustful. One woman told me that her husband announced he had decided to like her. Although he had always been very much in love with her, in his family that meant you were close enough to scream and express your frustration. His resolution to like her meant that he had decided to treat her as well as he treated his friends, whom he didn't yell at. He wanted to get along. Another woman announced to her husband that she would love him no matter 'how much he screwed up."

These declarations of affection may seem underwhelming and perhaps confusing, yet each of these statements marked a clear movement toward respect and mutual affection.

In the "Friends Again" Stage, each partner begins to use the information they gained about themselves in the period of self-examination. One begins to ask for compromise in ways that promote cooperation rather than competition. A partner may return to school or start a creative project with the full support of the other. Each partner may more comfortably accommodate a partner's need for friends that are not couple friends.

Many people worry when they hit this stage that they have lost their passion and spontaneity. At first, they feel more respect than passion for their partners. They are more careful and kind in their approach. They miss Stage 1, the Bliss Stage. The task in this stage is to move beyond mere civility to a deep appreciation and understanding of their partner. As couples work through their conflicts, their connection grows and leads them to a new stage.

Stage 5, the Bonded Stage is a stage of mutual respect and affection for someone very different from ourselves; a true couple stage. I believe this is the best stage, and often I encourage couples to struggle through the earlier stages because the end is worth it. In this stage, the partners each experience a deeper kind of love. Lucky couples reach this stage by the time their kids are five, but most reach it much later, hopefully before their kids' teen years when the pressure to act as a team is intense.

I rarely see couples in therapy at this stage because once they have hit stage 5, they have developed a mutual understanding of who they each are, who they are as a couple, who they are as a family, and what they share in common. Typically they are quite comfortable with each parent and each of the children having private time and developing personal interests and pursuits.

In this Bonded Stage, the couple's relationship shows striking flexibility. Partners can be silly and act like kids together, as well as be adults, plan together, and co-parent together. They can be passionate lovers. They share the excitement of each other's accomplishments. Each of them can also support and encourage the other partner at critical times, just as a healthy parent does when a child takes a risk, feels vulnerable, or gets discouraged. Both partners learn to shift these various roles in response to each one's individual needs.

When I meet families like this, it feels as if they are sailing on calm waters in a large, solid ship that has a clear direction. Their ship is home base. And although any one of them can leave it at any time to have fun, each family member will always want to return to home base and safe harbor.

The love you feel in the later stage recognizes that the other person has needs, desires, and interests different from your own. You love the other person and enjoy watching and helping them grow into who they are best suited to be. Recent research suggests that even very unhappy couples, like those stuck in stage two, who do not divorce, are much happier five years later when compared to equally unhappy couples that do divorce. It seems that it pays to hang in there and work it out when possible. That is great news.

How does understanding these stages help your marriage? Of course knowing that you are going through a predictable stage is reassuring, especially if you learn the pain has a payoff. It's comforting to know that other people have been through this and survived and thrived. People rarely have trouble knowing what stage they are in. Your friends or a good counselor can help if you aren't sure what stage fits. Finally, knowing the stages and how you work though them can help make the process easier.

While the stages are mostly sequential, people can move around a bit and sometimes go back and visit Stage 1 to remind them why they want the relationship. Some people slip back into Stage 2, the Differences stage, when under stress or when they aren't feeling good. However, once you have experienced a better stage, it is hard to go back for long.

ONE-MINUTE INTIMACY DRILL
When you both want more intimacy:

One person starts as a talker; the other is listener. The one who talks least takes the first turn.

The Talker says anything on his mind for 30 seconds while the Listener gives full attention, without interrupting, agreeing or disagreeing. The idea is to sharpen listening skills so after 30 seconds the Listener summarizes what the Talker said and the core feeling expressed. The Talker gives a score from zero to 100 based on how accurate it is. If the grade is below 95 percent, the Talker clarifies what he was saying and you repeat the exercise until the listener gets a 95 percent. Now you switch roles.

Almost immediately communication improves.

Tips for Getting Through the Stages Gracefully

- **Talk about what makes you happy** about your relationship.
- **Share small moments** and use them to remind each other why you believe you belong together.

- **Talk about your commitment** to make the marriage work and what you do to act on that commitment every day.
- **If you need a fix-it project,** improve yourself not your partner.
- **Aim for three to five nurturing gestures a day** like a pat on the back, a hug, a call, an email, an unexpected dry-cleaning pick-up or an extra thank you for regular jobs like filling the gas tank or paying the bills.
- **Hug, kiss and hold hands…a lot.** Look into each other's eyes. Let your partner catch you looking at them. The busier you are the more important it is to make contact.
- **Create family rituals** that support communication.
- **Don't pretend everything is perfect.** You have small children. Things probably are not perfect. Tell each other every day what makes you grateful that day.
- **Be there when it matters:** to celebrate successes, encourage risk-taking, and when times are tough. One husband charted his wife's moods during a difficult job search to give her perspective. Another reminded his wife that even though their daughter needed five surgeries, she would always be loved and not all kids have that.
- **Listen that extra moment** instead of jumping to conclusions that you know where this is going.
- **Share your deepest thoughts.** Write them down if you aren't awake at the same moment, but share them.
- **Embrace your differences.** Enjoy how they contribute to the relationship. Does your calmness balance his anxiety?
- **Make marital bonding as important as bonding with your child.** Don't bury your relationship under the demands of the children. Put your time and heart into taking care of your marriage and building your bond with each other, and your family's happiness will follow. When it gets buried anyway, notice that, laugh about it and talk about how you miss each other.

Note that all these tips are free!

9 Rage as a Signal

Although he thought their argument had
been settled at breakfast, Jim sensed that
Sally had some unresolved issues.

As I work with young couples with kids, I realize that rage and
the tendency to withdraw is a normal occurrence in long-term,
happy marriages, especially when children are young.

Before the birth of a baby, people feel that while divorce
would not be a good thing, they *could* leave if things got too bad.
"After all," they justify, "50 to 60 percent of couples do split."
Fortunately, the arrival of the first baby is often the time that
couples begin to feel a much deeper commitment to the marriage

and to feel much less like they will divorce. They tell themselves, "I couldn't do that *now* to our baby."

Ironically, with a greater sense of commitment comes a greater sense of entrapment. Each parent feels stuck as the challenges of the new baby and the new demands increase and the realities of what they have gotten themselves into gradually become obvious. They have never felt like this before. They assume either that the frustration they feel is the other person's fault *or* that they themselves are not meant for marriage. Each parent independently decides they must be inadequate or that their partner must be making them crazy. Neither is true, of course. Feeling trapped and frustrated, both partners may feel rage or resentment.

Some of you may say, "Why write about rage at all?" or "Isn't rage an awfully strong word" or "What does rage mean anyway?" If you feel you never have rage, ask yourself if you ever have the teeniest tiniest bit of resentment or irritation, and fill in the word irritation or resentment where I say rage. Ignoring all your resentment and never recognizing or discussing conflict often leads to boredom, affairs, or divorce. You don't need to feel rage, but couples need to recognize and work with, even enjoy, their challenges and differences.

It's important to talk about these feelings because too many people interpret their normal feelings of anger and frustration to mean their marriage can't, shouldn't, or won't work. In fact, if couples understand these normal feelings and handle them together, they are likely to go on to have stronger, more passionate, and happier marriages. Discussing differences or even feelings of rage and frustration is very different than merely venting rage.

Each couple manages frustration and anger differently. Many partners dance around the typical conflicts they feel about their baby and their partner and thus try to talk themselves out of feeling so negative. Some withdraw and avoid their partner when they are upset. Some yell. Some placate their partners and pretend to be happy, hoping that if they are nice enough their spouse will shape up and be nice in return. And I know several women (and men) who have just packed up and moved out, sometimes leaving the children when their partner didn't get "nice" in the way they imagined they could or should.

I also know one woman whose five kids were ages three through 12 when she snapped. She stopped abruptly in the middle of fixing dinner and just walked out the door and started walking down the center of her not-so-busy street. Now, her whole family of grown children quietly refers to this as her nervous breakdown. I think she was contemplating murdering her husband and possibly her children and decided to take a break. Fortunately, after an hour of wandering, she figured out what upset her so much and returned to mothering and housewifery. She is 90 this year and perfectly sane. She and I giggle about it now.

> *Each couple manages frustration and anger differently.*

When you are upset, in order to recognize your anger as a signal, you need to first understand that the person who is upset is the one with a problem. That's right, if you are mad, you are the one with the problem. That doesn't mean that you are wrong about what you see or want. You are probably right. You are also the very best one to resolve the problem because you are both more upset and more motivated than your partner to fix the problem.

The person who is upset is also the one who has the energy to make the change. Sometimes we waste this energy trying to get our partners to change by nagging, scolding, pleading, criticizing, using the silent treatment, or using many other unattractive strategies. These strategies, which are offshoots of rage, are terrible models for our kids and are better used as a signal to ourselves that we need to shift our approach.

Often, a wife drags her husband into therapy with her list of grievances in the hope that I, as a therapist, can get him to change. I can't. I can motivate her partner to make a few small changes, but for the relationship to change in a lasting way, she needs to learn how to influence her husband, and he needs to learn to yield to her influence and vice versa.

One lady, threatening divorce, forced her husband to come to therapy without her. She would leave me, the therapist, little encouraging voicemails about how brilliant I was in the hope that I could change him when she couldn't and didn't even want to try. But, eventually she came to realize that for anything permanent to happen, the person who wants change must change him or herself first. Gradually, the message-leaving lady began to come to the sessions with her husband. At first she tried telling him what a rotten father and inattentive spouse he was in the sweetest possible way. As we learned about her past and what her unrealistic hopes for the marriage had been, we began to get to work on a joint vision of what their marriage could be like that would be satisfying to both of them.

Be curious, not furious. Often, however, people's personal histories and expectations combine to fuel the anger in ways that make no sense to them. This is why I encourage couples to stay calm in the heat of the moment and try to figure out what events upset them. In other words: Be curious, not furious. Let me give you an example: Keith and June were a doctor and a nurse. June had come to therapy alone because she was surprised by a recent event. She had cut back her work schedule significantly to stay home with their first son. When their son was 18 months old, she and Keith decided to move to a larger house in a nicer neighborhood. The escrow date shifted again and again. Their move date finally landed in the middle of a ski trip that Keith and his buddies had been planning for several months. Keith's friends asked if he was going to cancel the trip. Keith asked June if she wanted him to cancel the trip. She assured him more than once that canceling wasn't necessary.

Of course, moving into a new house with an 18-month-old and the help of a couple of loyal friends didn't go as smoothly as June anticipated. When Keith called from the resort to see how she was doing, June was standing chest high in boxes with three people asking where things should go. "Don't bother to come home!" she shrieked at him, in a burst of rage that shocked her.

They talked the situation over when Keith got home. Keith apologized, but June went on feeling resentful for days. She didn't feel like having sex or being touched. This fight was on its way to becoming the fight that is recorded in maternal memory to be hauled out in all the wrong moments. "This is just like when we moved...." The intensity of her anger and the uncomfortable fact that June had told Keith to go skiing many times when he had asked, made it harder to see him as the insensitive, bad guy. June realized in therapy that she often took over in her family as the competent one, while others skipped out on responsibilities. She had wanted Keith to participate in their move but wasn't really aware of that until he wasn't there.

> *...people's personal histories and expectations combine to fuel the anger in ways that make no sense to them.*

Fortunately, learning to recognize when we are having intense emotional anger reactions signals us to stop and figure out what might be a hot button for us in a situation. Usually our anger reaction will seem out of proportion to the issue. Luckily for Keith, June, and their young son, June was able to talk through her emotions in therapy. She was then able to ask Keith to listen to what had been going on inside her head. To help repair the damage and reconnect, she asked him to participate in other moving-related projects, like filing changes of address and working on the landscaping. She continued to work hard to use her anger constructively. When she felt herself becoming upset, she learned to use her reaction as a signal to recognize her own needs and then ask for what she wanted before—not after—she became enraged.

Anger, rage, and irritation are like fire. A small campfire keeps you warm and gathers everyone together. A signal fire guides people. An accidental fire can scar you badly. An out-of-control fire can burn a house down, and an intense fire can scorch the earth and leave nothing in its wake, making it hard for new growth.

When you get irritated, a forest fire seems to erupt from a tiny spark. An emotional firestorm usually means that one of you is ignited or a trauma has been triggered by an event, a look or even a tone of voice. Often you are both quickly triggered at the same time because you care about each other. Bad memories are stored by emotion. When a tone of voice or situation triggers bad feelings or memories, you start working from your amygdala or part of the brain that is the trauma zone. When these bad memories sweep like wildfire through your brain, you are overcome simultaneously with every bad experience you had like this one. And you feel they are happening right now and not back then. So you are first hit with bad feelings from incidents between the two of you like "remember when you da, da, da" or "why does he (or she) always la, la, la…" You are also almost simultaneously hit with bad feelings from your family of origin and then perhaps with bad feelings from any previous relationship. You feel attacked, not just by your partner but by all the bad feelings you've ever had related to this look, tone, or situation. They seem to flood the brain as if a floodgate opened. These reactions flash faster than we can think logically. People attempting to measure this say that this trauma or emotional speed is six to 25 times faster than logic. We are emotionally flooded. And then we launch into defenses that worked for us as children, but don't work now. We fight, flee, or freeze based on what worked for us in earlier situations, regardless of what works with and for our spouse today.

Slow down. Most people caught in a flood of negative emotion need us to talk more slowly, more softly, more kindly and more gently, like we are talking to a frightened child even if they are yelling at us. We need better-than-good communication skills. We need special communication skills to reconnect with someone who is upset. I teach my couples to speak low and slow. Sometimes one or the other will marvel, "You said just what I say all the time but he (or she) got calmer and listened. Why?" I ask them to listen to *how* I said it. The trick is to learn to slow down, calm down, and speak gently when you or your partner gets irritated.

When you are mad at your partner, don't rush to respond. Take all the time you need, as long as your partner knows you're not ignoring them but cooling down and thinking.

When you first notice you or your partner becoming angry, take a minute to figure out what is happening. Were you sailing along happily when your partner said something harsh? Are you the one who fired the first shot? Are you upset with something your partner did or is something or someone else irritating you? Whose expectations were violated?

Use feeling words so they know that you understand they are upset like "Gosh, this is so frustrating" or "Don't you just hate that?" or "What is up, honey? You sound frustrated."

Do not give advice! The emotionally intelligent spouse, when the discussion gets to the final stage, is smart to ask, "Is there anything else you want to tell me about this?" And then, "Have you thought about what you want to do about it yet?" This question implies that you understand and accept that your partner may not be ready to move on yet. This phrase also suggests that you would be happy to move to problem solving when your partner is ready but you don't push your partner to go faster than is comfortable .

If your partner is mad at you, remain calm and listen. This is hard, but it is possible.

Usually, when couples want to discuss a conflict, I ask each partner to repeat back what the other has just said before stating his/her own point. Frequently this leads to comical results. The wife may say, "Let's talk about our relationship." The husband repeats back, "You think I have ruined your life."

If you can't listen right now, then tell your partner you want to be able to *really* listen carefully and suggest a specific time you can both focus. You could say, "Can we talk about this later tonight, so I can listen without being interrupted? I want to be able to really listen." My husband, Neil, says that men will need to have those words written on a flash card because no man he knows would think of that phrase spontaneously.

It is very important that you come back to the issue and bring it up at the time you suggested, so your partner will trust you.

If your partner is upset because you did not fulfill their expectations, do not defend yourself *no matter how reasonable you think your actions were*. Just be curious. "What did you think I was going to do?" Or, simply repeat back the feeling they expressed: "You were really hoping that I would remember, and it feels like I don't care about you because I forgot, right?" As you talk, try to get in these points too: "You are so important to me. I hate to see you so unhappy. What would you like me to do next time?" Or "what could we do differently next time?" If all that seems too hard, grab a big pad of paper and start making a list of each complaint without commenting. This is surprisingly soothing to an upset person because it communicates that you are taking them seriously.

You don't have to agree that you did anything wrong. Agreeing may feel dishonest to both of you. Just make sure you understand your partner's position, and let your partner know you care.

When you are the one who is frustrated first, use my favorite line. "I am not comfortable with this plan or this way of handling things." This is followed with either, "I need to think about it" or "I need to talk about it." If things are really tough, I say, "I need to write you a letter about it because if I start talking now, this discussion isn't going down a good road!" When I write things, my husband likes it because with careful self-editing I can remove the "you-moron" tone of voice and all my inflammatory, negative, shaming, complaining and blaming words *before* he reads it.

When you are mad at your partner, don't rush to respond. Take all the time you need, as long as your partner knows you're not ignoring them but cooling down and thinking. Later, I'll give you hints for expressing your anger in a constructive way. Right now, I would like to help you calm your rage as a couple with "truce triggers."

Michele Weiner Davis, best-selling author and solution-oriented therapist, first described *truce triggers* in her book, *Change Your Life and Everyone in It.* Truce triggers are behaviors that cause us to stop fighting. Most of us analyze to a gnat's eyelash what is causing a problem, but few of us figure out what gets us over our upsets and back on track.

Instead of analyzing what went wrong, take a look at your past fights. What made the argument end? How did you both get past it and move on? What worked? You can use these questions to analyze and plan how to get your conflicts on a productive path. Planning is like training in lifesaving techniques so you don't jump in the water empty handed and drown when the victim gets a strangle hold on you and tries to crawl up your body, drowning you both. Learning your truce triggers and planning how to handle repetitive conflicts are like lifeguard training for your marriage. I encourage my clients to *stop the name, shame and blame game* and try to *understand and plan* instead.

For some people, their truce trigger is laughter. Sometimes, startling someone works. Neil once *calmly* poured a beer on himself to demonstrate (as he explained when I froze mid-sentence) that "since I was so intent on dumping on him, he may as well dump on himself!"

Michele Wiener Davis points out that most partners don't necessarily have the same truce trigger. She likes a hug and her husband likes to be alone to recharge himself. They each needed to learn to give each other the trigger that worked. So her husband gives her a wooden hug, which makes her feel that he at least wants to resolve the problem even if he isn't ready yet, and she lets him leave to regroup by himself instead of following him from room to room to "finish this!" Learning to give what your partner needs, rather than what you think they should need, is critical.

My favorite couple therapist, Ira Poll, Ph.D., who has been happily married for more than 25 years herself, says that normal partners will disappoint each other. If you are pleasing your partner even 70 percent of the time, your marriage is doing very well. How the couple recovers from most disappointments determines the quality of the marriage.

Tips to Learn from Your Rage (or Withdrawal)

- Recognize your partner's raw spots and hot buttons, so you can approach them gently.
- Discover your truce triggers and your partner's.
- Agree in advance on a signal to start over.
- Create a buffer zone, a timeout plan that either of you can use when you are too upset or angry.
- Consider how to fix a problem next time rather than what went wrong this time.
- Create a signal that means you know this conversation/situation is going downhill and you would like to either help it go better or take a break.
- Consider specific behavior on your part to avoid the problem next time.
- Notice fights that you stop or discussions that go well. Congratulate yourselves, and see if you can work on issues that way in the future.
- Give support to your partner. A foot massage (or head, neck, or back massage) for a temporarily distant or silent partner will often change the relationship in a hurry. Having the energy to give the foot massage when you have small

children is the hard part. Some people find that by turning off the phone, putting the kids down and doing nothing but the foot massage, they feel restored themselves. If they then trade massages in their quiet time alone, things can get even better. Giving support is one of the best ways to receive it.

- Plan your life with a little leeway in it. Leave the kids with the babysitter or daycare and head out to the party an hour early. Spend that time with your honey. The goodwill from this prevents petty irritations from escalating into rage.

- Try to go one hour, one day, or one week without criticizing anything. I once clipped and saved a Dear Ann letter by a woman who saved her marriage by not criticizing her spouse for 30 days. I thought the woman should be canonized for sainthood for making such an abrupt and complete change. Yet, I know her method works. A single day without criticism generates incredible peace in my house, though I still find it hard to do. I have given this advice to many of my clients teetering on the brink of divorce. When they can refrain from criticizing, having a "no complaints" day (or better a week!) quickly brings peace for them so they can resolve deeper issues.

10 Where Is the Train Headed? Goals, Roles, Routines, and Resolutions

When my kids were young, simply getting through routine activities such as carrying groceries into the house, getting dressed or paying bills was an accomplishment. Our entire orderly life seemed to melt into a deep pool of urgent, yet trivial attention grabbers. Looking back, I wish that I had stopped to talk with my husband more about our hopes, goals, and values. I was often aware that our choices were limited because we hadn't planned. We could daydream, but didn't actually plan and execute. We longed for the spontaneity we had before kids, but we felt trapped in our daily duties.

When the kids were a bit older and I had time to reflect, I began to realize that although I had been clutching a date book and making lists for as long as I could remember, I hadn't really had much of a vision of where I was going. Neil and I had no vision together. We agreed about many things, most things actually. We both wanted children, but hadn't thought much about what we wanted to teach or share with them.

Confronted with the inevitable myriad of choices for raising a family, we wanted to do it all. We found ourselves saying yes to every invitation for our kids. Then we got so booked that I began to feel like we never really talked with each other about important things anymore. We just chauffeured the kids in different directions. It was too much. Our mistake was that we both assumed that the other wanted to do every activity without discussing it. Our assumptions and missed time together left us both feeling frustrated and out of touch. When we looked back at our choices, we wondered where our weekends and our lives had gone.

As I reflected and read more about this, I began to see that couples who had their acts together had mission statements, or general shared beliefs; they created rituals, for warmth and fun. Rituals created memories about what it meant to be a member of this family. They had roles, routines and rules to make life more comfortable and organized. This gave me hope that we could rediscover a semi-organized life that was more relaxed and fun. All we needed was a vision and some workable plans.

Goals, roles, and routines are also a positive way to get in tune with your partner. That way you don't need to argue, nag, and feel stressed to make snap decisions about what is important. Once agreed upon, each of these levels of structure gives a sense that you and your partner are working toward the same goals. They give your family an identity as well.

The best *mission statements* are short and focused on values. My favorite mission statement is: Live, learn, love, laugh. When compared to that standard, a lot of family conflicts simply recede. A dear friend's husband died a slow and painful death from a chronic illness. Yet the couple stayed happy and active with their kids right up to his death. After his death, she and the kids knew how to enjoy life. When my cranky, critical self begins to emerge, I ask myself if I knew Neil were dying in three years would this issue matter? A lot of stuff doesn't matter then.

LEVELS OF VISION AND ORGANIZATION

VISION AND MISSION STATEMENTS
Short, focused on values and meaning like: Live, Love, Laugh, Learn

GOLE SETTING AND FAMILY MEETINGS
Plans for next week, month or year to carry out visions like:

Where shall we go on vacation and how much will we spend?

Regular interests and hobbies

Saving money for college

A budget

ROLES
General job assignments like:

Who researches trips, who pays bills,

Who keeps the social calendar, who sends cards to friends,

Who watches the kids when, who does laundry,

Who makes dinners?

RITUALS
Reinforce sense of family, joy, and celebration, daily, weekly, and on special holidays like:

Planning holidays we spend with the relatives and friends versus "just our family."

Singing a special song at bedtime

Family dinners

Friday night neighborhood potlucks

Going to church regularly

Going out every year on Valentine's Day

Tea after dinner together

Watching sunsets on Fridays

ROUTINES
Habits that help us get through the day or the week smoothly like:

Paying the bills on the first and 15th,

Doing laundry one day a week

Changing the fire alarm battery on Halloween and April Fools Day

Who drives the kids to preschool a particular day?

Dad plays with Zoe while Mom makes dinner.

RULES AND CONSEQUENCES
Agreed upon discipline and self-discipline to support good habits:

If someone spends over budget, they get to do the bills.

Pick up before we go on an outing so the house is neat when we get back.

Taking a time out, if you can't be with people.

If you hit, you sit.

Unkindness means losing 15 minutes of a favorite activity.

STEPS FOR GOAL SETTING

Set Aside Times and a Place. Plan three blocks of *time without the kids or other interruptions*. An evening, a morning, and an afternoon spread over one weekend is great. Make sure your have some small breaks in the process. Here's how to proceed:

Create Three Lists Each:

- *Appreciation List:* Make a list of what you like about your partner, your marriage, and your life. Make it as long as possible. Expect your lists to be different lengths.
- *Problems/Opportunities (P/O) List*: Write down your needs, wants, and wishes. Then list them in order of importance. Try to state positively what you want to have or what you envision, not what is a problem or what is wrong. Use "I" messages: "I would like more meals at home." Not, "We never eat at home any more." Instead of saying, "I hate the way our kids behave," try, "I'd like our kids to speak more respectfully to us." This makes for a more productive discussion. Attack problems, not each other.
- These are issues that you want to problem solve with your partner. Add dreams, fun activities, and projects like: buy a house, trip to Africa, vacation in Spain, new career, good manners for the kids, or less clutter. *Dream Big!*
- Try to write your two lists before your first meeting or at least think about them. If you think about it while driving or in a spare (where?) minute you can jot down key words.

THE FIRST EVENING:

- **Start with positives.** Read your appreciation lists to each other first, and then enjoy dinner and the evening together. While this sharing doesn't take long, the goodwill helps you through the next steps.

The NEXT MORNING:

- **Share and combine P/O lists.** Have a pleasant breakfast. Find a comfortable and private place where you will have no interruptions. Take turns reading your dreams, needs, and wants to each other without interrupting. Combine your lists. This should take only10 to 20 minutes if you listen well, write down each person's list and do not interrupt.
- **Use your Best Communication Skills.** Stay positive or at least neutral. Some couples think the P/O stands for something besides problems and opportunities—especially if they are lost in rage. When you are making your list, imagine reading your list to a respected friend. Would they hear your wants and needs or a lot of anger? If you are too angry to talk about your wants or needs, consider counseling or working with a friend to reframe them more positively. If your partner's ideas seem impossible, too expensive, or ridiculous, just listen and write them down. Think of these as wishes not demands. Reflect back what your partner is asking without judging or criticizing, not even with your tone of voice. It is unlikely that you will each get everything you wish for, but you may feel closer knowing each other's dreams.
- **Ask questions** only to understand and gain clarification.
- **Prioritize the master list:** Agree on what you want to tackle first. If there are easy next steps for some items, agree who will carry it forward and when you will check back with each other. Do only one goal or topic at a time.
- **Brainstorm solutions for tough issues.** Start with the easiest issues and move to the more difficult. Try to think of five possible solutions together. This will give you more choices and you won't get stuck arguing that one answer is "right" or "best." Each person needs to contribute at least two of the five solutions. Be sure you give your partner's wishes the same attention you give your own. Come up with at least two crazy ideas. Have fun with this. Fun makes your thinking more flexible. Focus on win/win solutions. Write

down all ideas. If solutions come easily, move on to other topics. Table the tough issues.

- **Take a Fun Break.** Think about what you have heard. This break serves as a clear marker between listening and resolving conflict. Go out for lunch or for the evening. Exercise and have dinner and a date.

FOLLOW-UP: That Afternoon or the Second Morning

- **Evaluate the solutions.** Happy couples have very different styles at this stage. Try to look for solutions that are acceptable to both of you. Some couples decide to seek more information and reconvene at an appropriate time. One couple, happily married 30-plus years, who wanted to please each other had "secret ballots." After they had discussed every option, they would then write down what they really wanted on a piece of paper, slip the answers in a paper bag, shake it up, and then look at the answers. (Neither was a logic or a math teacher but it worked for them.) Sometimes couples just agree that they have very independent goals at this point. Others table the discussion. They need time to think so they simply agree to return, after they each have had time to meditate.

- **Set mutually agreed upon next steps.** Break the solutions down into real steps. Talk about which are the most important goals and which are the nice dreams for, maybe, later. Some goals will be primarily for one of you with the other playing a supporting role.

- **Discuss how you can work together and support each other.** What will happen first and in what order? How will you pay for it? How will you adjust your schedule to make it happen? Notice those items that are easy because you are already working toward them and congratulate yourselves.

- **Plan for follow-up.** Set a specific time to check in and say, "Well, what do you think? How did we do with our goals?" Plan follow-up for each project. A couple may decide to check in once a week on the relationship, if it is in trouble, or every two weeks on new habits for a child. Some put the goal list in the family meeting book and glance at it before family meetings.

- **Celebrate your hard work.** Congratulate each other on doing the process and agreeing on any tiny step together. Just taking one step together is an important milestone.
  - o Drink a toast.
  - o Frame your goals list.
  - o Put them in a memory book.
  - o Make love.

Neil and I have tried to recover from our total chaos by having family meetings once a week. We succeed in meeting about once every six weeks. For some people, goal setting is as natural as owning a planner or calendar. For others it is foreign and repugnant. I have heard planning described as a "restricting destroyer of spontaneity and true love." However, even the most recalcitrant doubters, once seduced into quote/unquote "planning" often become converts because of the tiny islands of peace and order that goal setting brings.

Goals. Getting started with family goal setting has always been the hard part for us. By the time my son was ten, he looked at me one day and said, "Mom how come we aren't like other families who just make a plan and do it?" His best friend's family is very organized. I didn't have an answer. Over time I have seduced my husband to do some measure of planning and goal setting by first asking that we make plans for our vacations together. Next, I started working on sharing calendars so I knew when we all had days off. Eventually we graduated to family meetings.

Family meetings to go over the upcoming week and reset the family course can be a good forum for establishing rules and expectations. When your kids are young, they can be brief, two-person meetings where you decide things like who is handling carpool that week.

People researching family meetings find that these meetings and especially family dinners are correlated with better marriages and better outcomes for kids, such as higher grades, higher self-esteem, fewer disciplinary actions at school, reduced drug use, and so forth. Here are the seven guidelines I have gleaned for a good meeting:

GUIDELINES FOR GOOD FAMILY MEETINGS

1. Start with praise;
2. Keep the meeting short;
3. Raise two issues at most;
4. Make meetings regular, but have an extra meeting as needed;
5. Serve good food or snacks;
6. End with positive feedback; and,
7. Do something fun after business is done.

Roles define who does what in a family. Many couples discuss and some even write down what their roles and their responsibilities are, although they don't always call them roles and responsibilities. Roles describe who is in charge of what to make things run smoothly. Sometimes, as children get a bit older, families divide the roles and responsibilities between parents and children. For example, some parents of teens let them each plan a day of vacation or handle the navigation and maps on a trip. People with clear roles are often comfortable with quite a bit of independent functioning and have a sense of self-respect. Giving kids specific roles fosters their decision-making abilities and sense of their own capability. This is great for both kids and couples.

A couple may need to review their roles, especially if their marriage is non-traditional and they haven't resolved who does what. Couples, who have a traditional view of marital responsibilities, and yet the wife works outside the home, may find that she is exhausted and they are growing distant. Spending time redefining roles to share work more equitably may help reduce that distance and give the overworked Mom more time and energy for sex.

ROLE SETTING

Each of you makes two lists.

- **Appreciation list:** Listing those activities your partner does to make the marriage work.
- **Problems/Goals list:** What needs to be done that isn't getting done? What do you want to work on first?

Agree on a time and place to talk.
Share your lists, using your best communication skills.
Prioritize your joint list.

Brainstorm solutions: Focus on what is likely to be fun for each of you and what you like to do. Remember not all wives cook and clean. I know urban families that have healthy meals delivered. Housekeepers are cheaper than counselors by a factor of 10, and cheaper than divorce lawyers by a factor of 40. Some jobs can be shared or alternated to help build empathy for the partner's role. Consider if there are skills you can trade with people outside the marriage.

Plan to switch roles for a while. Some couples take turns picking their jobs off the list.

Pick your favorite solutions to start. Come up with a plan that allows both of you to do what you like most.

Decide when to re-evaluate how the plan is going. Re-evaluate it in two weeks and then in a month or two. Some couples take another look every year or so.

Celebrate how well you work together.

Family Rituals. When you choose family rituals together, you grow closer as a couple. For families, a "compliment" ritual at dinner or an awards day once a week supports the family values that parents are developing in their children. Eye contact, a kiss, and a hug when you come home can be a family ritual. So is making a family memory book for each vacation. Choosing these rituals and supporting each other in making them happen strengthens the couple and the family.

Going to church or synagogue regularly is a family ritual that supports family values. I have had several wives who weren't particularly religious say that their spouses are calmer and closer to them when they go to church. So, the wives just remind the husbands how much better the husbands feel when they go.

Routines are more mundane but may be essential to the serenity of the family. Comfortable routines mean that important though not urgent things get done. You, your spouse and your kids can count on each other. Routines typically involve a schedule like who takes the kids to school and who picks them up on certain days, as opposed to the role of car pool chief who keeps track of who has to be where when. Some families do a monthly "coffee and all-nighter with classical music" for paying bills together. Neil is in charge of the family vitamins. He puts vitamins and juice out for us in the morning and packs vitamins for our trips. It is easy for me to forget, so I feel taken care of when he does it.

It doesn't matter what those routines are if they are comfortable to you both. In another family, Mom supervises baths and talking and Dad sings the good night song with them. Those very personal routines can be a kind of comforting glue that holds a marriage together. If you don't have or can't identify routines that make you both happy, you may want to consider creating a new one and trying it out.

While rules are a great child-rearing device, they are also marriage savers. If the two of you agree on the rules, you won't be second-guessing each other and having needless fights about why the heck you did or didn't do something. You present a united front that builds a sense of security for kids and parents.

You also won't be passive and distant because you are going along with rules that make no sense to you.

When partners have very different parenting expectations, they need to spend time initially creating straightforward rules and routines. Blended families, in particular, need rules and consequences from the beginning to maintain a kind of peace and to sort through the many conflicting expectations each member has from their previous families. Research suggests that functional, happy stepfamilies have more explicitly stated rules than conventional families. For example, no one comes in the parents' bedroom before 7 a.m. or, Dad and Step-mom have a date every Friday night.

Whether you carefully plan your routines, rules, roles and goals, or grow them slowly over time, they help to reduce conflict and confusion and create peace and fun.

Tips for Creating Goals, Roles, Rules, and Routines

- **Brainstorm** all the things, both big and small, that the two of you want for your kids and your family. Most couples will already have some goals, roles, and routines in place.
- **Notice visions, goals, routines, rules, and roles you already have** in place first. Are they long-term goals or rules and routines? If you have lots of rules and no goals, consider setting goals, and you may need fewer rules. If you have a vision but no steps to get there, consider your roles and routines.
- **Consider whether your routines support your values and vision.** Do your spending habits and time commitments support your values?
- **Take small steps.** I like the couple who puts a dollar in the jar every time they make love and then use the money for a trip to Hawaii. That's a good example of small steps leading to a large goal. With kids, it is especially hard to make large changes rapidly, so focus on the small steps.

- **Post your goals** or mission statements where you see them often or put them in your PDA or planner.
- **Get an attractive family journal** and record the date and notes of your meetings. Use it to note the changes and progress you make.
- **List rules and consequences in a family journal** and watch how they evolve over time.
- **Start with a plan that is fun** so you are more likely to do it and keep it up.
- **New Year's resolutions** can be at any of these levels and still be meaningful.

11 Normal Problems—Real Solutions: Balancing Work, Love, and Life

Moms and Dads feel guilty about an endless list of things: Not spending enough time with their kids, letting them watch too many videos, giving them too much fast food, shrieking at them occasionally. Parents need to balance work, love life, and time for themselves. For moms, perhaps the most pervasive guilt feelings come from trying to juggle jobs and kids. "Mommy, why can't *you* be our nanny?" a precocious seven-year-old once asked, leaving her hardworking mom momentarily speechless. Stay-at-home moms feel guilty that they aren't earning enough or being a good model of achievement for their girls. Women feel this conflict between work and home more acutely and earlier than most men. Typically, they begin to think and worry about these home vs. work conflicts before their children are born. According to survey results, men don't report thinking about this until they are older than forty. It's like men slap their forehead and go, "Oh no, I forgot the kids!" Sometimes their wives slap their heads for them, verbally of course.

Feeling a little guilty is actually a sign of a good parent. Conscious, aware parents have an acute sense they are making choices that profoundly affect their children.

There are several ways that happily married couples set their work-family priorities. The traditional approach is for the wife to stay home and give the kids plenty of attention, and the husband to go to work and bring home the money. Married parents today often both work and hire a nanny or take the child to day care. Some couples try to share all tasks equally. Even more rare, are Mr. Moms, the stay-at-home dads. Although couples can discuss these options in advance and will probably choose an approach before the kids are born, the reality is that people often change their minds once they have kids. And they frequently regret or second-guess their choices a lot! Dedicated career women suddenly quit their jobs; committed homemakers pine to go back to work or have a small escape. As one lady commented, "I want a job just so I can wave my hand, cheerily, and say 'I have to go to work. Ba-bye.'"

When the husband takes an "It's up to you how much to work and how much you want to be home" approach, he encourages his wife to make an independent decision. Sometimes this makes the issue easier, but this solution still carries the seeds of potential conflict or disconnection. The wife may feel abandoned because he isn't participating in this important decision. Sometimes the husband says, "Choose whatever you like," then becomes resentful when she chooses not to work. Or he goes along but feels tense and worried under the financial burdens.

Men rarely discuss their conflicting desires to be the sole breadwinner, which can be an ego booster, versus the very tangible benefits of two incomes. The down side is that sole breadwinners often feel left out while Mom exerts, as one guy put it, "executive control over parenting." As more than one traditional working dad has said to me, "She makes all the decisions. The kids know it. She only asks me when she isn't sure what she wants to do." A traditional mom may feel she should be the one to make parenting decisions because she is the one who is with the kids the most.

Moms worry about these issues and dads worry less so, unless they struggle with the notion of the Mr. Mom arrangement. Mom often feels the need to talk about the choices she is required to make almost daily regarding childcare, school, and time for her career or herself. Most likely, Dad isn't going to appreciate her angst. He will feel that these discussions are endless, uninteresting, and pointless. Even if he does get it, "What am I supposed to do?" he wonders. After all, he feels he knows his role; he is supposed to go to work and make money like Dads have been doing forever. She often envies the freedom society has allotted him and his guilt-free take on parenting, especially when he seems so clueless about her angst. The contrast is clear when he leaves for work: The kids kiss and hug him and wave sweetly. She leaves for work and the children cling and cry. Or she lingers and feels melancholy after she drops them at day care on her way to the gym, wondering if she is doing the right thing.

Of course, some moms drop the kids off with relief so they can retreat to the quiet and calm of the office. It doesn't take long to realize that most jobs are cleaner, quieter, and neater than raising kids. Withdrawing into the relative comfort, safety, and quiet of work is tempting. Long hours at work usually mean that you miss time with your partner as well, cutting yourself off from the emotional support you once had from your spouse. Work begins to seem like a haven not only from the kids but also from the emotional issues brought up by trying to co-parent.

Many childcare experts feel that from birth until two-and-a-half is a time when a parent has the greatest impact on a child's personality and intelligence. Although many parents feel this means they must stay home, stimulation is the critical issue for developing a child's IQ, EQ, and social skills. Some research suggests that having mom out of the home and away from the baby no more than about 30 hours a week is optimal. Mom's happiness with her choice best predicts her child's happiness and success. There are no right or easy answers.

So how do you start a conversation about these issues with your spouse? For women, the best initial conversations about these issues may be with girlfriends. Most women experience these issues and will be inclined to discuss them at length without feeling the need to take action today to fix the problem.

Talking with sensible, happily married girlfriends can help you sort out your feelings before approaching your spouse. For example, after bouncing my feelings off my girlfriends, I realized I needed to work at least part-time. I am far too bossy and controlling. I would drive my kids crazy if I spent too much time around them. They would never learn to be independent. I always loved the Harvard research that indicated that the most successful adults could be identified at age three by the fact that they could ask another adult, besides a parent, appropriately for help. The other studies that reassured me were those saying that the family does best when mom is happy with her choice to either work at home or work outside the home.

Another problem in most marriages is giving up "couple time" to the kids. My mother always said that the best parents are lazy parents. Her theory, as I understood it, was that lazy parents don't jump up every time their kids need something. So, lazy parents, theoretically, have more time for each other because their children learn, maybe by the time they are 25, not to interrupt them when they are together. What follows is the antidote to all the self-help advice on how to be the perfect parent. The current high standards for parenting lead to low standards for marriage. Helicopter parents, who are always hovering, tend to raise kids who aren't used to planning and taking responsibility for their own lives. Not the desired result. The irony is that having a healthy marriage is a great gift for your children and yourself. While it is easy to say take time for your marriage and a date night every week, the reality is much harder. When couples are courting, making time to talk is given careful attention. The idea that you would lose your connection seems strange, even impossible. If you tell someone without kids that couples who actually talk only about fifteen minutes a day are rare and special, they will think you are unrealistically pessimistic. However, married people with kids think you are special if you *do* actually talk fifteen minutes regularly.

Yet, in truth, carving out quality time with your partner can be done. I have met couples who snuggle in bed for 20 minutes after the alarm goes off, or have a cup of coffee or tea together after dinner, or always talk before or after a late night show. They call each other at lunch. They establish "date nights."

They are a lot happier than many other couples. And, their kids end up feeling safe from divorce.

Couples who connect routinely see habitual time together as reassuring rather than rigid. They certainly feel something is missing if more than a few days go by without establishing the connection. When inevitably they miss their talk time, they do something soon to restore it.

Career-minded women quickly recognize the need for childcare. Both women and men are much slower to recognize that childcare is necessary to support the marriage.

My mother always said that the best parents are lazy parents.

We had friends who claimed they would be long divorced without their beloved nanny and housekeeper "to blame things on and do the messy jobs we both hate." Good childcare can mean valuable time together. However, often couples assign responsibility for hiring, training, and firing household help and childcare to the mother. Unfortunately, this can reinforce Dad's position as an outsider. Discussing child-care needs at different stages throughout the marriage and sharing responsibility for selecting and training the caregivers, means you are likely to be happier with each other and your decisions.

I had always assumed we would have a live-in nanny until I was ready to hire one, and my husband said he couldn't stand the idea of having another person in the house. I was glad he was so direct about his needs. That caused me to reorganize our plans and I have never regretted it. Years later, when the housekeeper kept popping back in the door one more time while we waited impatiently to have an intense discussion, I suddenly understood why he had wanted to protect our privacy.

The cost of childcare is a significant item in the family budget, and needs to be discussed in advance to avoid conflict. If one of you doesn't work outside the home, you may assume you don't need childcare. Wrong. Skimping on childcare may be skimping on your relationship as a couple.

If cost is a major factor, consider a babysitting co-op. We tried one and it was great. This is an inexpensive solution and a great way to meet nice people. Usually a co-op is a group of people who earn credits babysitting for other families and spend credits when other parents sit for them. You will need the cooperation of your spouse if you want to use it for date night, because you will have to reciprocate.

Whatever you decide, revisit and re-evaluate your decision together often. Expect that the arrangement that works today may not work in a year, or even a month. Kids' and families' needs change. The happiest families adapt with these changes.

Tips for Becoming Comfortable with Parenting Choices

- Answer the questions above for yourself.
- Ask your partner the questions only one at a time rather than doing them all at once, so you can really consider the answers and not flood your partner. You don't want it to seem like an oral exam.
- Compare the answers. Be sympathetic.
- Look for differences as well as similarities.
- Consider doing a journal or list of things that you both admire and things you both would rather not bring to your marriage.

Part Three

Travel, Holidays, and Other Crises

12 When One Parent Travels

If having a baby is like tossing a hand grenade into a marriage, as writer Nora Ephron once quipped, then a spouse's job that requires frequent travel adds the land mines.

A mom, left behind when Dad travels, often grows resentful because she didn't sign up to be a single parent and yet often it feels as though she is. Traveling spouses often feel lonely and left out of the family, as though they are just there to send a paycheck. They feel even more strongly than most husbands that their opinion doesn't seem to matter except perhaps in an advisory capacity. As one traveling dad put it, "I have all the authority of a teenage babysitter!" Both kids and the stay-home parent (who isn't always Mom) will say, "Stay out of it because you are never here!" so the traveling spouse often doesn't feel like a real parent. On the other hand, sometimes Dad is so eager to be accepted when he gets home that he spends lavishly or gives in on everything to be popular.

Frequently, both kids and Mom, if she is the full-time parent, are cool and distant upon Dad's return, not because he has done anything wrong, but because they unconsciously feel as if they can't count on him because he will be gone again soon.

If you are prone to jealousy, worries about flings loom large while your spouse travels. Meanwhile, stay-behind parents feel that all the housework and childcare have been unceremoniously dumped on them. Women often feel they can't complain because of the money the husband's traveling job provides, which allows her to be home with the kids, as she originally wanted. Both parents struggle with feelings of resentment. Both feel they should be receiving more gratitude from the other mate.

Good discussions about the relationship, the workload, or anything of real substance seem impossible because neither parent wants to discuss anything heavy or even bring up minor trouble—like a broken washing machine—in the precious time they have together. But, you need to stay connected and avoid these resentments.

A common, unpleasant experience in families with a frequently traveling spouse is the phone call home at precisely the wrong time. Junior is in the bath, or it's story time, or you are trying to mediate a dispute. Although telephone interruptions seem trivial and annoying, solving this problem is the first step to creating a feeling of connection.

Schedule regular telephone times to call and speak each day—just the two of you—like in the morning before the kids are up or evenings after they are asleep. Use that time to share about your day and to iron out any difficulties or plans that need to be made. Regular calls create a routine that is comfortable for stay-behind parents, which makes them less likely to be cool and distant. Often one or both members of the couple may want to save time or money by not checking in, but do not realize the potential problems over the long haul. I remind them that time on the phone is much cheaper than counseling or a divorce and encourage them to choose some methods of supporting their relationship that feel right for them.

Call at another time to speak with the kids to keep your connection with them. *Their* time is as important as your "couple" time. Kids' ability to relate on the phone develops as they grow. Don't expect much in the beginning.

Use fun reminders to help keep you focused on each other, rather than letting resentments build. For instance, attach some meaning or phrase to the wedding ring like, "Every time I look at my wedding ring I think of you and what you are doing for us and our kids." This works both for the person out earning money and the one working with the kids.

Have a special item of jewelry or underwear that you each wear as a reminder to feel close during your absence. One couple used the phrase, "Our house" which meant to them, "We are doing this travel only until we can save enough for the house we want."

Leave behind a card or tuck one in a suitcase to say, "I am thinking of you."

One husband I knew would call his wife on her cell phone when he got in late after a business meeting so he didn't wake her because she fell asleep early. When she woke up and listened to his message, she could hear the time he called and know he was safe and how he was feeling. Then they could talk together when he woke up.

Very young children quite often miss the traveling parent and complain to the stay-at-home one, creating additional stress between the traveler and the stay-at-home parent. At a very early age, the child sometimes can't even understand that the missing parent will be back.

Contented children help the home parent tolerate the traveling parent's absences better. Couples use an endless number of truly creative ways to overcome this separation anxiety for their child. Some of my favorites are listed here.

Tips for Overcoming Separation Anxiety

- One dad calls home every night to read his kids a story from a copy of their favorite book, which they are holding at home. As the kids get older, longer serialized stories work.
- A mom made a laminated photo of Dad and son together for the son to carry, sleep with, and talk to, as he needed.
- A traveling mom put a recorded message and a comforting favorite song on a play-back tape in a stuffed toy.
- One dad made a video of himself before a month-long trip to Paris.
- One family uses a calendar to cross off the days until Mom returns as part of the bedtime routine.

- One daddy fills a special huggie bear with his hugs and kisses so the kids can go hug and kiss the bear when they miss him.
- Another mom gives her son a big lipstick kiss to carry in the palm of his hand.
- These are all great things for your child, and your spouse will probably feel great that you made the effort to keep that link alive.

13 Kids, Couples, and Vacations: Taking the Kids

Trudy and Tim, clients of mine, described the vacation from hell with their kids and Trudy's mother. In three short days of record-breaking heat on Labor Day weekend, they learned that their son could crack his head open twice on the same coffee table and the "suite" they booked at a resort was one room and so tiny that they needed another expensive room for Grandma. They learned too late that Trudy's mother didn't like to leave the hotel and pool, and that their infant son, overtired from an 11-hour day the first day, could indeed whine and cry for four hours straight. The second day, the oldest child, age six, was deeply disappointed because Granny and the baby limited so many of the family activities. When all this became apparent, Tim (used to traveling with a backpack and no itinerary) announced he would never go on another family vacation again.

While I sympathized with them, I also giggled, even though I don't generally laugh at my clients' troubles. I laughed because I had heard so many vacations with kids turn out this way. I told them about a trip another couple took with two grandmothers and two kids to Costa Rica. Both grandmothers adored their grandchildren but preferred sightseeing to watching them. The grannies wondered why they weren't invited on the next trip, despite dropping a lot of hints.

I suggested to Trudy and Tim that they were lucky they had only spent three days learning these lessons. Most couples take more trips and endure longer trials. Fortunately, Tim had been on many fun family vacations as a child, which helped put this disaster into perspective. He knew that trips are the *stuff* of life-long memories. Even if children are too young to remember the trip themselves, they see the photos years later, and sense their place in the family's history. But the reality is that while traveling with kids is a trip, it's hardly a vacation. Making it enjoyable for everyone takes creativity and planning. In counseling, Trudy, Tim, and I started to figure out how to make their next experience a big improvement over the last.

I began by sharing some of what Neil and I had learned the hard way. We began flying with our kids before they were a year old, making our biennial trek to visit family. My only rule was to travel where the doctors spoke English, so I could communicate my hysteria should the need arise. Fortunately, our calamities weren't health related, but calamities we had. A porter once accidentally kept one of our boarding passes, so we were denied access to the plane on Christmas and spent an extra thirteen hours in various airports before arriving at our destination. On another trip, Clark's carefully packed formula didn't make a connection, and we arrived in Alaska at 11 p.m. with no formula. Good thing our taxi driver knew just where to get formula in the middle of the night. When planning a trip, it was hard for us to imagine that it could be harried and not at all relaxing, a microcosm of all the clutter, chaos, conflicts, and lack of spontaneity that we had hoped to escape.

We soon learned that traveling with kids could be both a time for great bonding and a time for marital trauma. The bonding occurred when we worked as a team to get the kids through security, on the plane, and—we hoped—to a fun destination and home again where we could coo over pictures in a memory book.

Some couples fantasize that they will have a romantic getaway with the kids in tow. Not likely. If you expect to relax when you take the kids, you will be greatly disappointed. If you plan ahead, you can create a little down time. For example, if you travel with friends or family, you can trade fixing meals and childcare. If you chose an all-inclusive type vacation with meals and childcare provided, you may sneak in some relaxation, and maybe even romance. Some realistic (and experienced) couples take family vacations and don't expect to have romance until they take their private weekend. Or as the kids get older, they have a private week when the kids are off with grandparents or at camp.

Others take grandparents or nannies on vacation. This can be great if your expectations match. Consider your agenda first: Do you just want their company or do you actually want to them to help? Are they healthy enough to truly enjoy the vacation or are they likely to slow you down? Are they good travelers and used to adjusting to what may happen? Will they need or want naps or free time away from the rest of you?

Vacation planning can be the toughest when children are infants. At young ages, Mom may be reluctant to separate from the baby even if you bring a nanny. She may also be reluctant to leave the child with a stranger at a resort that provides childcare. Dad may not see the point of taking a nanny, and the nanny can be a problem. One couple I knew took a nanny to Hawaii. She turned out to be a fish out of water because she wanted to take care of the baby 100 percent of the time. They had to struggle to get time with their baby! Very awkward. Another nanny wanted to party every night just when Mom and Dad needed her most.

As you can see from these examples, the parents need to talk both with each other and with the nanny or granny, if they decide to take them. They need to be particularly clear about what they hope will happen on vacation and how much relaxing they can reasonably expect.

With a comfortable plan, infants can be the easiest to take on trips. They sleep a lot, so you are both able to relax away! Their food is portable and easy to deliver, especially if you breast feed. Anything is a toy to an infant. Sucking either breast milk or a water bottle reduces dehydration and, more importantly, takes away the ear pain on landing, which is usually the main cause of crying.

Children ages nine months to two or three years have the most difficulty traveling by plane or car unless they sleep. Active kids this age hate to sit still. They don't understand why they should. Their feeding habits are disgusting to other passengers—messy and difficult. Toddlers don't really understand how to inhibit their actions at that age and think "no" means, "Look quick. Mom's getting upset." Of course, it helps if you follow the parenting advice in most books for this age and teach your child that "no" is a signal that Mom or Dad are going to stop an activity. This requires teamwork, and kids this age need constant supervision, which doesn't translate to a relaxing vacation for you.

> **Children ages nine months to two or three years have the most difficulty traveling by plane or car unless they sleep.**

A dear friend and veteran of cross-country flights swears by taking kids on the red-eye flight. The plane may be nearly empty and your child may sleep the whole way. If the child is prone to airsickness and you feed them very well early in the evening hours before the flight, they may have nothing to throw up during the flight. There is rarely a need for any messy feeding since it is their sleep time. The red-eye flight is rarely canceled and you can stay in a motel if it is. This works best if you can tolerate sleep disruption, which I can't. I end up looking like yesterday's newspaper and feeling worse, so I developed daytime flying strategies.

Bring along a light blanket. You'd be amazed at the uses. I was given a thin open-weave, airy white blanket that worked as a breast-feeding shield, an extra layer on a cold plane, and could wipe up spills in an emergency. Usually though, I draped it over the stroller or car seat handle when Clark slept. This blanket discouraged overly friendly strangers from reaching out, touching him, and kissing him. When Clark woke up, he could see through it and would let me know when he wanted to be uncovered, without screaming. I fantasized that it reduced the spray of viruses from sneezing strangers as well. Two years later, Xander and I happily used the blanket, and it has been passed on to cousins.

Breastfeeding makes it easy to fly with a baby. Although I think breastfeeding is great, some people can be quite hysterical on the subject of breastfeeding in public. I developed a couple of tricks that made breastfeeding easy and private. I often wore a light, semi-loose fitting sweater with another cardigan or soft jacket over the top. Xander could happily bury his head under that combo and my breasts offended no one. He seemed to like the solitude. I also had the loosely knit blankie that allowed the kids to peer out while others couldn't see in. Xander loved the privacy. He would come and snuggle for comfort under my sweatshirt against my blouse long after breast-feeding was over. Most airports and many planes have diaper-changing tables, but it helps to bring your own Velcro safety belt to strap the baby snugly in case the safety belt is missing.

Past breastfeeding age, bring your own food. The airlines will rarely feed you when the kids are hungry, and the kids won't eat what they offer anyway. I once spent two hours strapped in my seat with a baby and a toddler on the Denver runway waiting for take-off. This is not an uncommon occurrence and having your own food is a lifesaver. Breastfeeding several years eliminates some of the feeding issues.

At this age kids love presents, and they don't even have to be new. Just wrap anything they haven't seen in a while. They also love to trade little toys with others. We would let them pack a tiny backpack with older, inexpensive toys, so we didn't worry about losing things. They were happy trading and sharing with others.

Kids ages four to 12 may still have considerable difficulty sitting still for long but can be distracted with new books, games, and toys. If your child has special difficulty sitting still, traveling in the early morning hours or late at night while they sleep may continue to be your best bet. While we ordinarily avoided wholesale use of electronics, we found long car trips and airline rides could be vastly improved with electronic games, movies in the car, and other pursuits—especially when each child had his own game or activity. As they got older, a miracle occurred and they actually began playing with each other so we could talk.

Here are a few more "traveling with kids" tips—learned in the trenches—to preserve your marriage.

Tip #1 Even if it is while you are waiting to board, talk together about who is going to watch which kid when, who is going to sit where, and who is carrying what so that you have a strategy. At least one of you will need to be on duty all the time after a child begins to walk and talk.

Tip #2 Try new types of vacations: The joy and the challenge of kids are that they induce you to try new vacations, vacations that you never would have dreamed of going on before kids. But heads-up: deciding what constitutes the perfect family vacation is often a source of marital conflict. Each partner often has a particular vision–sometimes based on childhood reality and sometimes on unfulfilled fantasies. Dragging a city girl to family camp or a dude ranch can be a tough sell. Make sure you listen carefully to each person's dreams and fears and compromise if the visions are vastly different. Some couples alternate: a camping vacation followed by a room-service luxury vacation. I have even known couples to combine them: Death Valley followed by Las Vegas.

Tip #3 Vacationing to see family can be relaxing if cooking and housekeeping duties are shared with other family members. Some couples do great "family" vacations with friends who have kids, and can share some of the chores and childcare. We have taken car trips with other families and let the kids decide who rides in which car. Even toddlers loved this arrangement and were on better behavior with their buddies in other parents' cars.

Some people *visit old family friends or aunts and uncles* so that they can go to a child-friendly house where their kids are welcome. Just be sure you are truly welcome. Friends of ours brought a toddler to our house three years after our kids were out of that stage. As I caught their son climbing a fence at the edge of a 20-foot drop, I realized what great friends they were to have entertained us when our kids were that age.

And that's not all... *Don't rely on a brochure:* Be sure to talk to someone who has been to the place you plan to visit. I once arrived at a destination to learn that "laundry included" meant once a week if it didn't rain. Another time, we thought a trip to the Galapagos would be fabulous because our young children loved animals. A phone call to the tour guide quashed this idea because children under eight weren't welcome.

Another thing, *include the kids in plans.* As soon as my kids could walk, I gave them little backpacks and let them begin packing whatever would fit that they wanted to take. (Remember, you will end up carrying these bags when they are asleep, so keep them light.) Limiting toys to one backpack that they packed had many advantages. By age eight, they were wearing their backpacks and helping me with my rolling suitcase, so I was empty handed as we strolled through the airport. Quite a change from pushing a double stroller with two car seats in it!

One more important thing, *share your plans and expectations for car, plane, and restaurant behavior with your child before the trip.* "Library voices" and "good restaurant behavior" are much easier to explain beforehand than later with a growing line of angry people behind you. For car rides, some families adopt various rules, such as you must alternate the favored seat or you each have an assigned seat you always take, and so forth.

Sometimes we *have the kids make the rules for the trip.* When the kids help articulate the rules, they are more likely to cooperate and the rule will be phrased in a more interesting manner. Almost any plan works, as long as Mom and Dad agree with it. But a plan is a must. In the old days when just the two of you traveled, you could wander about making spontaneous decisions. Not anymore. Though some couples feel a plan ruins their vacation relaxation, some plans improve the traveling part. Trust me, you can enjoy some spontaneity after you arrive.

Quick Travel Tips with Kids

- Talk about the trip with your spouse and kids in advance. Focus on what you expect to enjoy about the trip as well as behavior expectations.
- Plan how and who will entertain the kids and what the rules will be.
- Discuss how your child's age or changing interests might make this trip different from the last.
- Consider what job to give the kids. Depending on their ages they may carry a tiny back pack, help with bags, plan the itinerary or be in charge of directions, or hailing a cab.
- Figure out together how you can have couple time alone.
- Ask what has been challenging for each of you about previous trips and talk about what to do to make this trip better for each of you.
- Plan how each of you will get relaxation time to yourself on the vacation.
- Ask each other if you are planning to alternate watching the kids or use another form of childcare.
- Allow extra time each step of the way because traveling with kids always takes longer than you think.
- Review the plans on the ride to the airport.

14 Birthday Battles, Christmas, and Other Catastrophes

Birthdays

Everyone knows supermoms who plan and organize perfect parties. The invitations arrive early. Everything has a theme.

I used to do these parties—well, as close an approximation to them as a founding member of Nitwits Anonymous can possibly manage. The results were disastrous, although the kids enjoyed them enormously. My husband complained grumpily that I spent too much money and that our children would be spoiled. As another birthday drew near, we would each have our own depressions. I would do all the work for the kids, thinking I was doing Neil a favor to take over the job, all the while feeling lonely and unappreciated. Neil would show up late for the party, hang back, and generally have a terrible time. I would, of course, be frustrated about his lack of participation. We viewed these parties from completely different perspectives.

The *crowning party* had a pirate treasure theme. I had read about sprinkling the table with gold wrapped chocolate coins and making treasure boxes. My husband, in a token gesture of helpfulness, said he'd seen some at the corner convenience store. I was running late with both kids in tow. I ran in the store and located the coins at the checkout counter. Just as I was about to pay, my younger son said, "I have to poop *NOW* Mommy!" I hurriedly paid the man, grabbed the coins and rushed for the exit.

The coins looked gorgeous and everything went pretty well, despite the fact that my husband decided to build a child-size table for the kids one hour before the party so the guests arrived to the buzz of a saw and flying sawdust. Shortly after everyone left, while we were still basking in the glow of the festivities, a mom called. She cautiously told me the gold coins that I had thought were chocolate were, in fact, condoms. "I was pretty sure you hadn't intended to start sex ed that early!" she said giggling. I reflected on the startled look of the clerk when I cleaned out his condom supply in such a desperate rush. Fortunately, all the mothers I called to warn found this hysterically funny.

After that party disaster, I decided to send my husband to the store the next time to buy the party favors with the kids. I'd been doing the buying alone for years, to a chorus of criticism. I had splendid visions of the kids running riot in the party store with him alone and me being truly appreciated. At the last minute I weakened and we all went together. Two parents and two boys were a lot better than one parent and two boys in the party store. Dad ended up spending more than I did. The stuff was totally tacky and without any theme, but we had a good time together and all the kids loved the stuff.

For the next party, I asked Daddy's advice every step of the way. As years of parties passed, the kids reinforced Dad for his "good judgment." He got so into giving birthday parties, he even insisted at one point on giving a party for a friend's child who had never had a party because his parents were both afraid to do it.

Holidays

But here's the thing; holidays can be more difficult than birthdays. Because family responsibilities change so dramatically with the advent of children, when holidays hit, couples can be plagued with hassles and crises that put them at odds with each other. Time, energy, patience, and resources run out rapidly. I see too many grownups in therapy who have sour memories of their childhood Christmases. When I get cranky with my spouse or kids, I try to remember to ask myself if this is what I want them to remember about a holiday. This helps me pull it together and get back on track.

Here are a few thoughts on how you can cope and create connection with your partner and children during this challenging time:

Talk with your husband or wife about what is meaningful to them about a particular holiday. You will probably have very different wishes depending on what you loved and hated about your own childhood holidays. Don't be surprised if what makes a perfect holiday shifts dramatically once you have children and keeps shifting as they grow. Ask each other, what happened when *you* were a kid and what do you want for *your* children? What really makes this a holiday? Is it surprises represented by presents? Is it the link to their religion or spirituality? Is it the spirit of giving? Is it the music? Is it the chance to express gratitude to all the people in your life who have brought you joy during the year? Is it the chance to be with family? What are your partner's worst memories and biggest disappointments? Discuss what is realistic and what is Hallmark nonsense.

> *Don't be surprised if what makes a perfect holiday shifts dramatically once you have children and keeps shifting as they grow. Ask each other, what happened when you were a kid and what do you want for your children?*

Recognize that it will no longer be possible to have a "perfect" holiday once you have kids unless you scale your expectations to make your holiday kid friendly. Having kids suddenly makes these questions loom larger. A holiday that was never that important to one partner may be extremely important to the other after kids arrive. When partners see holidays differently, defining these holidays after kids may suddenly become a struggle. One solution is to create a cross-cultural holiday. Many mixed faith households, for example, include a menorah and a Christmas tree. The important thing, though, is to hear each other out. Create your own family's holiday rituals by asking each person to share an activity that means the most to them and build from there.

Rituals are particularly important in newly formed stepfamilies. They do not have a history of resolving this year by year. Now they are suddenly presented with new children and new expectations and two or more sets of new grandparents and extended families. They have two sets of memories: those from the family of origin and from the family of divorce—some good, some bad.

While you're building rituals, consider starting a holiday tradition that bonds you as a couple that will be meaningful even when the kids are grown and gone. Buy at least one gift or spend one time together that is just for the two of you. During the holidays, I know couples who have a Christmas dinner date for just the two of them. Others buy a nightgown or negligee each year for her and some goofy sex thing for him. Whatever you do, the idea is to exchange something private that's just between you two.

And don't forget to *create new traditions with your kids.* Think about what kinds of memories you want to have about Christmas when you look back with your children in five or ten years. When they write that eighth-grade essay on "my most memorable holiday," what do you each hope they remember? As they get older talk with them and add little traditions or change the plans to fit.

On a more practical level, *get a calendar and write in what you are going to do when.* Think about what you both consider important and decide which jobs to divide and which to share. Schedule the shopping trips with individual children to shop for siblings, or make something together for gifts.

Decide when you are going to wrap. Schedule social dates only with people you really want to see. Once you see how full the calendar is, and that you have too much planned to actually do it all, you will start making choices more easily.

Right off the bat, *talk about your holiday finances* so you can avoid spending January lamenting your excesses or blaming each other. This can be a big strain on your marriage. If your child won't get that dream present because you can't afford it, see if other family members want to chip in. Do tell your child if you think Santa can't afford it. By the time children are old enough to long for really expensive presents, they are usually old enough to know that sometimes Santa has a budget and may not be able to bring everything on their list. It is better to be realistic before Christmas than to substitute something they do not like and send a message that what they want is wrong or that they are unreasonable or bad for asking.

Better still, *eliminate some things.* I know of one family who skipped exchanging the glitzy presents when the kids were older in favor of a big relaxing restaurant dinner. *Our* best plan was that we would alternate spending the holiday with Neil's large family and mine. Each of my sisters fell into the plan as well; we meet on Christmases falling in even numbered years and do the alternate Christmases with our in-laws. This eliminated a lot of stress because everyone could count on the deal.

Whatever you eliminate, *the aim is to create meaningful, fun, and memorable time.* We make a family ritual of buying the tree and having hot chocolate. I make hot chocolate and Neil plays Christmas music for the tree trimming. Our kids would never let us take that special night off the calendar. They do try to avoid watching his favorite holiday movie *again!*

Another possibility is to consider *teaching kids to remember others.* While acts of charity are time-consuming, they make memories and build character. Your church, synagogue, or school may have great ideas for craft parties or giving opportunities so you don't have to organize it all by yourself. I know a group that does a Giving Party where kids make Christmas decorations and collect money for a homeless shelter. In another group, kids make things to sell to each other, and the money is donated to help abused children. The kids deliver the money and visit the shelter.

A word of caution: Such volunteer work, while laudable, can stress your marriage if you don't do it as a family, it's poorly organized, or you don't make sure it is something you both support enthusiastically.

You can also *use your village to de-stress the holidays.* Trading baby-sitting with another couple can give each couple shopping or date time alone. Bail out a friend with a new baby by buying a gift she needs to give to someone else. She may return the favor later. Appreciate the magic that others bring to the holidays. Invite someone you know who has a special talent to be in charge of the music or family plays this year.

Keeping presents in perspective makes the holiday easier. Taking into account the developmental age and stage of your child when opening presents makes more fun for everyone. An infant or toddler is often more interested in the wrapping than the present. Allow plenty of time for gift opening. Don't rush. Adults may need help slowing to a child's pace. Opening more than one or two presents can be overwhelming to a small child. A large extended family or older sibs often can't wait to see what the little one's reaction will be, but it's often disappointing when the little one just wants to tear into whatever is next and shows little interest in her new toy. The Hanukah tradition spreads the presents over several days. This works well because it fits with what young children can handle, and gives kids a chance to comprehend and enjoy their gifts.

Talk this issue over with your spouse and make an agreement in advance about how you will manage gifts so that you have similar expectations. A common conflict would be the person who likes a giant stocking filled with many inexpensive presents married to someone who likes one thoughtful, expensive present. Any compromise comfortable for each of you will work. If you expect differences, the times you agree are a pleasant surprise.

Let's face it; older adults often love genuine appreciation more than gifts. *Consider thoughtful notes instead of gifts* for some people. Teachers have real experience with well-intended, but strange presents. I discovered that teachers love notes of appreciation, sometimes even more than gift certificates, especially if you quote your children or have them help you write them. (And they may appreciate it even more if you send a copy to the principal.) Older relatives and friends, who have everything, enjoy notes of appreciation and school pictures or photos of them with your kids. I express my deep gratitude to my kids and husband for being cheerful about the grueling cross-country trip to visit my relatives, to friends for their friendship, and to co-workers for just being great people. Appreciation feels great, and doesn't bust the budget or take a lot of time.

Remember, stay realistic, flexible, and *do not strive for perfection.* Following these key principles makes it easier to delegate and ask for help when your kids are small. If you are less concerned about making everything perfect, you can feel more comfortable asking for and appreciating the help you get. Talk to others about the holidays to get ideas about how they keep their perspective by not overspending and over-stressing. In the end, those details do not matter as much as how you and your family enjoy the holiday together.

Give Yourself a Break: Holiday Tips

- The best breaks are hug breaks. When you are rushed, stop and give your partner a hug. Hold hands. Kiss and hug your kids.
- Appreciate. Tell your partner all the things you are grateful for. Tell your kids what you are proud of. Write them down and post them. Tell people what you appreciate about them everyday. It's free. It's quick. And it means a lot.
- Stop and read a Christmas story together even if every little thing doesn't get done.
- Skip a party if you don't really want to go.
- Don't send the cards one year, or skip the handwritten notes.

- Watch Christmas videos like "Prancer" or "The Grinch Who Stole Christmas" with the kids instead of doing the next thing on the list.
- On your master calendar, have one day in the holiday season when nothing is scheduled.
- Consider the dreams and expectations of family members and grandparents, aunts, uncles, and cousins when deciding on activities and discuss them well in advance—around Thanksgiving—so you are all on the same page.
- Schedule special Christmas couple time on that master holiday calendar.
- Schedule "just our family time," for special Christmas rituals.
- If your spouse is gone a lot, take a day off work by yourself to shop.
- Schedule a babysitter and go with your spouse early in the morning or late at night when fewer shoppers are out.
- Have a cup of tea, breathe, and focus.
- *Most importantly,* enjoy your family and spouse *your way.*

15 It's Not Working: Normal Sexual Dysfunction

Most couples are staggered by the rapid changes in their sex life as a result of pregnancy and the birth of a baby. When the baby is newborn and you and your partner are alone and awake, it can seem either like heaven or an awkward meeting with a stranger. Pregnant women and new moms often experience little or no sex drive. Easy, spontaneous sexual encounters disappear and sexual responses change dramatically.

Many wonderful pregnancy books discuss possible changes to expect in your sex life. All agree that there is little uniformity in how women and men react. Sex can stop or sex can become more intimate and personal as each partner begins to recognize the individual reactions of their partner. Familiar sex may be replaced by a different kind of sex that is more deeply satisfying.

Often women feel that they will never be slim again. I gave away a pair of my pre-pregnancy jeans because I was sure I had somehow gotten the wrong ones in my closet. I truly believed that I could never have been that small and certainly never would be again. But, miraculously, I returned to size and my wise friend, who had laughed at my craziness, simply returned them to me when I lost the weight. Neil swore up and down I looked great even though I gained 50 pounds, bless his chicken (but prudent) heart. Only when I lost my pregnancy weight did he confess he had doubts I would ever get back to my old size. Many men have this fear.

Women can have very different reactions to their own pregnant bodies. Some feel fat and lumpy and others revel in their own voluptuousness. They enjoy finally having cleavage in pregnancy and love to flaunt it. Dad's reaction can have a lot to do with how they respond to themselves and to sex. If you comment on the softness of a woman's skin, it focuses her attention away from her worries about her body size.

Occasionally husbands have trouble being attracted to the post–pregnancy body and need to talk about that with a counselor or a friend. Even if this is the case, avoid negative comments about a woman's figure to her. I have seen marriages struggle for years, even after Mom had regained her figure, because Dad had commented negatively on her post-pregnancy body before she lost the weight.

Some new parents have trouble having sex with their partner because instead of a lover they now feel they are in bed with a mom or a dad. And they don't see moms or dads as sexy. Generally women have less trouble with this issue than men.

BABY BLUES By Rick Kirkman and Jerry Scott

Other moms feel they have to give up wearing sexy clothes because they are now moms and the *other* moms don't dress like that. This may be related to how other mom's dress, such as wearing practical, comfortable, stain-proof clothes that work around kids. They may feel less sexy because they aren't dressing in a way that is a turn-on to themselves—or to their husbands.

Avoid these traps by sharing your fantasies and feelings, and developing a relationship that is a turn-on for both of you regardless of size. Some couples work out a signaling system with special nightclothes that mean, "I am interested tonight," or try new sexual experiences when they are rested up. But other couples grow resentful around this issue. Remember to take time to reconnect because the quality of your post-baby intimacy— more than sex—will determine the happiness of your marriage for the rest of your life.

New fathers have their issues as well. Witnessing childbirth, although supposedly a joyful, bonding experience, has rendered more than one new dad temporarily impotent or at least reluctant about having sex if it leads to repeating their birth experience. Overly graphic doctors' explanations of death and danger, even temporary injunctions against sex after birth, can chill the ardor of many a male who is sincerely fond of his wife.

Couples may find leaky breast milk or a crying baby jolting them out of their lover mood and into their parent roles. Some couples experience these feelings together, but in other cases one partner feels the contrast more sharply than the other. As one mom put it, "When you have a baby and a two-year-old sucking and touching you all day long, even cuddling with your spouse at the end of the day can feel like an invasion." Sympathy, understanding, and some adult talk-time without the baby, help to dissipate this feeling of invasion, and eventually sex becomes more appealing.

Many ordinary physical difficulties interfere with good sex. Pain should be promptly explored with your doctor. Do not continue to have sex that hurts. Practice will *not* improve the situation. You can very quickly develop an aversion reaction that will make you both avoid sex for years. Until you solve this, use alternate forms of pleasuring. Medical expertise in the area of painful intercourse is quite uneven. Seek a second opinion if the doctor:

    a.   doesn't help in one or two visits,

    b.   tells you to just go ahead and have intercourse and it will pass or

    c.   implies that it is all in your head.

Despite all these difficulties and insecurities, this can be a wonderful time to experiment. Share sex stories and fantasies, oral sex and massage. Be careful that whatever you do is mutually satisfying. The partner performing oral sex, for example, can easily begin to feel resentful if it only goes one way. Talking about what is mutually satisfying can lead to an even richer sex life because it opens up the couple to communicating about sex techniques they may not have tried before.

The sexual path may go astray if the wife now expects Dad to share more of the workload and is constantly disappointed. The new dad may have trouble being attracted to someone who is frequently disappointed in him and constantly criticizing. He will be revived after a few days of absolutely no criticism or expectations and a bit of romance.

Do-it-all supermoms may feel that they have no interest in sex long after the doctor's warnings have expired and the baby has passed the disruptive toddler and preschool stages. Regularly, in our group practice, we see couples where the husband drags a reluctant and overworked mom into therapy because she has no interest in sex. If the couple enjoyed sex before the baby and there was no pain with intercourse, we often prescribe what we call "housekeeper therapy." We ask the husband and wife to hire a housekeeper for a month prior to continuing therapy. (Housekeepers by the week are cheaper than therapy in California.) Generally this resolves the "sexual problem" and reduces our waiting list.

Even if you work around these various normal challenges to your sexual relationship and keep close communication, your preschoolers' activity level and inquisitiveness may become another roadblock. You may find yourselves so horny that you are picturing where in the house there is a closet big enough that you could lock yourselves in for a few moments without the kids noticing you're gone. At least you will be checking out closets and trying to find a slice of time together and that is a good feeling.

The bottom line is that sex—more than any other area in a relationship—stirs up the most varied and unpredictable responses. Feelings change throughout the pregnancy and in the early years after a child is born. Some level of sexual problems, mainly reduced frequencies and desires, are the norm rather than the exception in this period. Yet, couples can, and sometimes do, emerge with a sense of greater closeness and communicate better than before. They discover new things they consider sexy. They can enjoy each other in ways they never knew were possible.

When I told my husband in a burst of excitement that I had found a whole series of books on *Romantic Weekends in Southern California, Northern California, New England and Points in Between,* he said, "Does it come with a baby sitter?"

Romantic weekends are obviously best when you both are excited about the place you go and about each other. A year or two after having a baby, most couples gradually discover their marriage needs new spark. Enjoying each other sexually on command during a romantic weekend may be difficult due to the hassles and issues discussed earlier, and the fact that it's hard to stay awake for more than two extra minutes. Young couples may not be able to afford the baby sitter or the expensive weekends that are advertised in glossy magazines. But somehow you need to carve out time without the children to reestablish your sexual relationship.

If funds are short, consider, as the British say, "vacationing on the premises." In other words, stay at home and have your kids stay somewhere over night or for the weekend with granny or a friend. Use the time you would spend packing and traveling to spiff up your place like a bed and breakfast. Do the laundry or hide it from sight. Line up some indulgent activities that you could never do with the kids around like perusing good massage books or watching stimulating movies. Since you aren't paying for a hotel room, consider having joint massages at home. Or just play hooky from work together and do something you both love, like having an affair with your partner.

> **Start by asking your partner what makes him or her feel loved.**

Romance, then sex: Think of reestablishing sex as a two-step process. Romance, then sex. Most new moms are the easiest people on the planet to romance.

Almost any gesture that is complimentary or helpful toward the baby, the mom, or the housework is romantic to a new mom. And your wife will be the envy of every woman in the neighborhood who sees you helping or complimenting. Anything that is the least bit caring will help create a good mood. Great eye contact will work wonders. So will seeing her as a woman and a person rather than simply a mom.

Before the baby she may have been the one who remembered special dates or planned special evenings. But now, if she is too tired and distracted to do this the relationship drags, and the new dad feels dumped. If the new dad takes over generating some of the romantic moments in the relationship, his gestures can carry the couple through these rough initial months. Likewise, any words of appreciation go a long way toward helping the couple through this period.

I encourage both partners to try to do one romantic, appreciative gesture for their partner a day, even if it is only a touch on the cheek and full eye contact. When you are exhausted and frantically busy, just one gesture a week will help jumpstart the action. In the interest of efficiency, I encourage couples to focus on caring gestures that really mean love to their partner.

Start by asking your partner what makes him or her feel loved. People give astounding answers. I remember one woman who was married to a highly educated professional. This fellow felt neglected if she hadn't opened and sorted his mail when he got home each day. That was love to him. She loved to chat and felt loved when he talked to her and she thought the mail was irrelevant. But when she did the mail, he felt loved and ready to chat. Everyone likes their quirks indulged, I suppose.

If a couple is in trouble emotionally in their relationship, partners often *don't know* and can't even make a good guess what pleases their mate. Sometimes I help couples make what I call Care lists of things that make each of them feel loved. Often on the list they will discover that there are things they already do that the partner enjoys and hasn't mentioned. If your partner is list phobic, ask them to give an example of when they felt the most loved by you. This will give you ideas about what works. The inquiring partner enjoys hearing what the partner likes and can focus on those things more. I then encourage them to try things from the caring list and discover what else works.

The positive environment created by these caring gestures lays the groundwork for good, open, honest communication and good sex. While this seems like, and is, a slow and indirect way to approach regaining a great sex life, I encourage couples to see it as an investment in their future.

When you both feel ready to try sex again, it may be best to start with whatever is familiar. Double-check that your partner is ready and inquire, more than usual, about each other's comfort as you go along. Take your time. Good sex leads to *more... and better...* sex.

If there still seems to be a barrier to restarting your sex life, consider what might be going on between you and your partner. Perhaps, one of you may be fearful of having sex because the other wants more children. The reluctant partner just may be too overwhelmed by the child you have and all the change that has come with that to feel warmly toward intercourse and what that might produce. This is a common issue when couples have difficulty resuming sex after the birth of a baby. You may need to establish birth-control boundaries so that you can both feel comfortable again having sex.

Another problem some couples find is that after the birth of the baby, or after years of familiarity, what used to be exciting just isn't anymore. In the process of moving through the stages of marriage, one of you may become more eager to try something new. It can be very hard to discuss the desire for more variety with your partner. Just saying that you would like to try something else implies that you aren't happy with what is. Not a good thing.

Partners have better luck when they say something like, "I feel so safe and secure with you and I am grateful for that. Feeling safe makes me wonder if we are close enough to experiment a little more. I have read about things others have tried, and I think you might love them. What do you think?" Saying I have read or seen things on TV is important because many partners jump to the conclusion that you have been learning from a new teacher or talking with some one besides them. Also not a good thing. Helping your partner feel better by exploring new ways to be together is a good thing.

If your partner seems repulsed by sex, consider counseling. Often this is a signal that there was early sexual trauma and a trained counselor can help move you past that problem. With counseling, you may achieve a better sexual relationship than you had prior to having children.

WILL I (SHE) EVER BE THIN AGAIN?

Uh. Yes, no, maybe so. This question terrifies many a new mom in our size-obsessed society. Some dads are anxious as well. Many a new mom can't have sex simply because she feels she isn't thin enough to have sex. "I can't bear to have sex because I can see the wrinkles in my tummy." There is nothing as discouraging as stepping on the scales after pushing a watermelon out between your legs and finding you haven't lost a pound! But breast-feeding and nine months may do the trick.

Jumping up and down to take care of a baby burns more calories than most Americans do in their sedentary jobs. However, when either of you allows the new baby to completely disrupt your previous exercise routines, you risk gaining weight.

I won't presume to give you diet advice. Too much has already been written on the subject. Remember, no one can make anyone lose weight. There are helpful and unhelpful ways to respond. My clients offered these suggestions:

- Do not *ever* use the word "fat." Fat is one of those loaded words that people can say about themselves, but no one else can. I can call myself fat. You can't.
- Do not comment on my weight even if I complain about it constantly.
- If you want me to lose weight, spend time with me taking walks, rather than making drinking and eating our fun time.
- Do not make cookies or other "treats" a reward.
- Regular sex is a form of exercise that burns calories. Seduce me with talk and massages.
- Support my efforts to go to the gym or walking with friends, either financially or by offering to do chores so that I can go.
- Go on a diet with me and say it is for your health. Stick to the diet.
- Praise my attempts to go exercise and walking. "Atta girls" help.
- Arrange some childcare and time to walk with me.
- Clean up the dishes after dinner so I don't eat the extra food off the kids' plates.
- If I gain weight, comment that I look down or a little unhappy (not fat!). Ask if there is some way you can help.
- Ignore my weight and tell me I have beautiful eyes, skin, or hair.
- If I lose weight, tell me I look fabulous and that you love to see me so happy.

Note: If I obsess constantly about my weight and eat candy alone like an alcoholic or take un-prescribed medication to lose weight, I am probably sick and I may need therapy. High-sugar food and white bread can be an addiction just like alcohol.

One clever, loving husband, whose wife drove them both crazy with weight worries, told her in front of me in therapy that it never stopped him from wanting sex. She blushed and soon lost weight gradually on her own. Great answer. Take note.

Tips for Fostering Romance and Sexual Closeness

- Expect your sex life to change because it will.
- Talk about your worst fears about sex during pregnancy, like giving the baby brain damage with your enormous penis and laugh together. Then comfort yourself that it is impossible.
- Get a book on massage and try something new.
- Get massages together. (Tell your masseuse who is pregnant.)
- Talk about what it is like to feel fat and tired…and a father.
- Practice alternate forms of pleasuring like sharing fantasies, looking at pictures of pregnant ladies, oral sex, and massage.
- Try to keep the satisfaction mutual even if you drastically modify your routine.
- Ask around and see who actually thinks their sexual relationship is better since pregnancy and kids. (You will become interesting at dinner parties.)
- If sex hurts, see your doctor. If it doesn't get better, see another doctor.
- Give your wife a lot of reassurance about her looks during and post pregnancy.
- Cuddle and stroke each other a lot.
- When you are reading baby books, take some time to read about sex and massage.

- When you are out to dinner, make lists of the ten most romantic weekends you can imagine.
- Ask your partner what you do that makes him or her feel most cared about and most loved.

- Ask what else might make him or her feel your care and concern.
- Take a re-vote each anniversary on your favorite caring gestures (and sexual positions)!

16 Affairs: Preventing and Repairing

Few events in life are more heartbreaking to an unsuspecting spouse than an affair. I can remember laughing with my friends about our unnatural attraction to the repairmen who came to our houses in the few quiet moments when our spouses and kids had left in a whirlwind of noise and demands. Accepting and laughing about your escape fantasies can help avoid affairs.

However, too often couples don't have this awareness. Instead they focus on what is wrong with their partner or blame their partner for couple conflicts, making it easy to rationalize an affair. The partner having the affair reasons that it is not good for the kids if the parents divorce so perhaps an affair would keep the family together. They could also have sex and/or romance and still preserve the marriage—they think. "Who would it hurt?" Any rationalization works.

In order to have an affair, women first feel that their marriages aren't good or lack intimacy. Men, on the other hand, are more likely to say their marriages are happy—yes, happy—while they are having an affair. After the affair, when they are asked again, many men and women often decide that their marriage was no good in the first place—even though they rated it as happy before or during the affair.

Men are a little more likely to have affairs than women, and statistics on who has affairs vary dramatically, depending on how long the couples in the sample have been married, the definition of an affair, and who is asking the question (and in front of whom I suppose). Some estimates say that in as many as half of all marriages, one or both partners have affairs. Suffice it to say that any long-term relationship is at high risk for one or both partners to have an affair at some point in the marriage.

Not surprisingly, the sheer exhaustion and lack of sex drive make the period just after the birth of the baby an unlikely one for women to be the ones to have an affair. Women are more likely to stray when their kids reach preschool and are a bit more independent. On the other hand, if men are not involved with the mother and the baby in this period, they are more likely to have affairs during pregnancy and in the first two years after the birth of the baby.

Stepping stone affairs are most common. They are related to the "trading up" process that author William Doherty talks about in his book, *Take Back Your Marriage.* These relationships assure the straying partner that someone out there finds them attractive and, as they head toward divorce, they won't face a lifetime of loneliness.

A "charmer" initiates another type of affair. Charmers often feel unsuccessful in their career or life at the time they begin an affair. They need to feel better about themselves by making someone else feel special and needed. Both men and women are particularly vulnerable to this type of affair when they are in the "Who the Heck Have I Married?" stage. In the charmer affair, affair partners who have been seduced are those who are more likely to define the marriage as *happy* if asked early in the liaison and, paradoxically, to report the same marriage as having been *unhappy* when asked later, provided that the illicit relationship has proceeded well.

The "Can't Say No" guy is closely related to the charmer. Men will often describe being unable to turn down a proposition, as though they have been taught that a gentleman can never say no to a lady. The availability of an affair partner is seen as an opportunity—like the lottery—not to be missed. Availability holds the most attraction for someone who didn't see himself or herself as attractive or popular in high school. This feeling lingers despite the fact that the man may later be quite successful and attractive. Others (although less frequently, women) simply don't know a nice way to say no and assume that what the partner doesn't know won't hurt him. I have had men and women tell me that, "*The sex* *wasn't even that good.*" They just went along. Of course, such indiscretions usually hurt both partners and the marriage. However, marriages often recover from this type of affair if it is discovered or disclosed fairly rapidly because the affair partners have rarely invested much emotional commitment.

Mr. "Duck Hunter" is another type of fellow aptly described by Frank Pittman in his classic book on affairs called *Private Lies.* Some men, and more rarely women, have a duck hunting mentality. They make a sport of seducing as many people as they can. To some men, affairs are a sport learned at their father's knee. They were often taught by Dad about his affairs or even asked to help hide them. The son learned from his dad that such affairs have nothing to do with his mom and, therefore, nothing to do with the son's attachment to his wife. Rather, these men feel affairs affirm their masculinity.

When these men grow up and try this in their adult life, they are quite upset if the wife chooses to leave because of his affairs. Contemporary women just aren't as forgiving. This is particularly sad because these men often describe their marriages as happy and their wives as wonderful. They have great difficulty understanding why *their* wife isn't more understanding, as *his* mother was. The advent of AIDS and public awareness of other STDs (and perhaps the equality of the genders) have somewhat reduced this type of affair. The only way to prevent these duck hunter affairs is to avoid marrying someone who has this attitude and has a parent with a history of multiple affairs. However, men rarely confess to this history, although often a family member or close friend with a stricken conscience will warn the bride just before the wedding.

Finally, there is the "emotional affair." I see this most often in people who were molested and maltreated as children. Often, particularly if someone they knew and trusted molested them, the victim doesn't enjoy sex even after trust and love have been established in their marriage. Then, the normal pressure to have sex leads to emotional distance of the victim. This is because the victim doesn't understand his or her own sudden post-commitment disinterest in sex. The molested or abused partner may seek an outside safe (non-sexual) relationship that is intimate and emotional.

In these cases, the non-molested partner (usually, but not always, the man) may be in love with a wife who doesn't like sex. This makes him feel both deprived and inadequate. He first struggles with establishing a relationship and then engages in a long-term affair with a woman who doesn't want an intimate relationship but does want sex. Neither partner wishes to leave the other, nor do they want the marriage to end. When either the spouse or the affair partner presses for a more permanent relationship, the marriage goes into crisis.

Professional intervention can help the couple work out the problem. Molested and abused partners are often quite relieved to learn that their loss of interest in sex is related to their childhood trauma. Once this is established, they can work in therapy more comfortably.

Although affairs may seem to be fun in the beginning, people rarely anticipate the hurt and havoc they eventually wreak on all parties, including the people who break them off. Kids suffer because a parent can't be fully present when his or her heart and mind are lost in an affair. I have watched the fallout of affairs for years in clinical practice, and the best advice I can offer is to try to avoid them if you want a long-term happy marriage. If you feel like having an affair, seek counseling before you act. This may seem like obvious advice, but it probably won't seem obvious while it is happening to you. If your marriage does experience an affair, seek help from a good counselor familiar with Shirley Glass's book, *Not "Just Friends."*

Before affairs even seem like a possibility, discuss the boundaries that are comfortable for you both. Will you go out to lunch or dinner with friends of the opposite sex? What about professional contacts? How close will you stay together at parties? Will you go to parties, theater, or movies alone or with others of the opposite sex? What are the comfortable boundaries of sexual talk and flirting? What are the intimate things you will keep private and what are the intimate things you will you share with others? How do you feel about chatting online with the opposite sex? I don't feel it is necessary to impose my boundaries on my clients. However, if they choose very loose boundaries, like exchanging sexual partners, I point out that the people who wrote the book on open marriage ended up in divorce. Also, daily, or almost daily, contact with a member of the opposite sex that isn't primarily work related can spell trouble.

Tell your partner, "If you have an affair, I will kill you." Just kidding. People who are quite comfortable in their marriages will often say something direct, simple and to the point like, "If you have an affair, I will hang your cojones on the clothesline." Unfortunately, if one partner's character or nature is to avoid conflict, then he or she may feel completely unable to talk to the other about these feelings when an attraction does begin. People are notoriously inaccurate about what they will do faced with their partner's attraction or affair, even though they may express a strong opinion.

Try to notice signals that indicate you or your partner are especially interested in someone and talk calmly about that interest. We can't help who we like or love. We can help what we do. Some people just assume that because they would not have an affair, their partner won't either. But if one partner is quite unhappy and has trouble expressing this, or expresses it repeatedly and is ignored or shut down, an affair begins to feel like a logical alternative. The spouse just drifts to an affair partner to avoid conflict or criticism, instead of choosing to struggle in the relationship any more. If you start seriously contemplating an affair and can't talk to your spouse about it, go to therapy and save yourself a lot of grief.

The majority of people who engage in affairs are conflict avoidant. That is, they just don't like to fight with the one they love. They are nice people and charming when you meet them. They are often communicative and self-disclosing. They can find an affair partner easily. They can be quite articulate and even argumentative about a variety of topics. But they have trouble discussing or delivering bad news about the relationship to their partner.

They have trouble making comments like the following, which could send up a flare for help: "I am not feeling close to you." "Our relationship isn't working." "I am feeling attracted to other people." "I am lonely." "I am missing you." "Our sex life could use some spark." "Our relationship is flat. Could we try something new?" "Sex scares me." Or "Sex hurts." They do not want to hurt their partner's feelings. They may be afraid to drive them away by speaking the unpleasant truth. But these comments are all going to be easier than having to say that you are having an affair. If you are having any of these feelings, use them as a signal that your relationship is in trouble. Either talk to your partner or seek professional help to figure out how to best to approach your partner.

> **The majority of people who engage in affairs just don't like to fight with the one they love.**

Many couples with difficulty talking about differences and conflict in the relationship act out in ways that destroy their marriage even when they agree on their values and have nearly everything else in common. Here are two examples that didn't end so well.

Judy and Jim were both gentle, devoted, fun parents. They each arranged their work schedules to tag team each other so the kids were always with one of them. They were proud their unusual hours meant their children had no nanny or child care support person. Unfortunately this arrangement left them almost no time for each other. Both parents agreed on the rules and standards for their kids. Their three children were the center of their lives and possibly the most beautifully behaved preschoolers I had ever met.

Unfortunately, Judy had an unacknowledged need to talk things out and avoid conflict. Before kids, they had plenty of time to talk, without Judy having to ask. Judy felt loved when she could share her day, each day, with Jim. Judy's father had abandoned her family in divorce when she was quite young. Her mother had met and eventually married a calm man who liked to talk things over, which was what Judy wished for in her own marriage.

Jim came from a deeply committed family in which "actions spoke louder than words." The chores you did for the kids and one another and what you each provided financially communicated *caring* in Jim's family. Otherwise he didn't need to talk. He felt that Judy demonstrated love when she went along with what he wanted to do.

Although Jim didn't physically hit his wife, he was willing to argue any point until Judy finally saw it his way. She felt she just gave in to stop what she called his unrelenting "hammering." After kids, Judy seldom acknowledged her need for time with Jim to just talk until she blew up in a rage. Then she let Jim know just how inadequate he was in the communications department. He politely ignored these blow-ups because he felt she just needed to "let off steam."

She was a prime candidate for the attentions of an unhappily married man at work who loved to talk and listen. This man had had multiple affairs and many family difficulties, but he was a great listener. Sadly, she soon became involved in an intense affair. She felt terrible guilt because her affair was outside her own value system. With this extra guilt, she felt even more hopeless and paralyzed about asking for what she wanted in her marriage.

When her new man was hospitalized for drug and alcohol rehabilitation, she sought counseling. But it was too late. By the time she realized this new man was not Mr. Right, she had already divorced Jim. Her children were learning to live in two separate houses. Although Jim and Judy were good parents, they handled conflict in a destructive way, alternating between polite over-compromise and hostile explosions.

Clearly Judy and Jim had very different expectations about compromise, love, and connection. Each assumed that because they had so much agreement about their children that the other issues would get better. Judy didn't realize how unhappy she was until someone started to listen. Jim didn't realize she was *really* unhappy until she asked for a divorce. Then he was ready to work on it, but Judy was already deeply involved in the affair. By the time she realized her affair partner was not the answer, Jim was finished trying and had angrily moved on. How much better it would have been if Judy had said she missed having fun talk-time and Jim had learned to listen sooner.

In other couples, neither partner ever blows up. When post-kid frustration triggers a fight or flight response, they flee into an affair. Anger and frustration are underneath a calm, disconnected exterior. Doug and Meli were the center of a large circle of friends. They organized great parties, outings, and vacations for everyone. They were viewed as the perfect fun couple. At first, kids just added to the mix because they organized great things to do for families with kids. Both participated in caring for the kids and they had lots of help. But neither was very good at asking each other for what they wanted.

When conflict came up, it was smoothed over. Although they problem-solved little things, they didn't talk about the frustration and distance they felt after kids. They would sometimes have long, grinding, rational arguments that left them feeling empty. They began to avoid each other and those arguments. Neither understood what was happening. Both were polite, and yet bored with each other. Being with other people became a welcome distraction from the undercurrent of conflict and unhappiness.

Meli began having emotional rather than sexual affairs with a series of people and eventually found someone. The marriage ended because they "fell out of love" although each will tell you how great the other was. They went to therapy briefly, but Meli was already so deeply involved with the next person that they didn't continue.

Both couples—Jim and Judy, Doug and Meli—blamed the affair for the break-up of their marriage. None of them realized, however, that the real culprit was unresolved conflict. I have seen marriages survive even after very serious affairs because both partners sought help and took responsibility—not only for the affair but also for their own needs. And, they worked together as partners to rebuild a strong marriage.

The best way to prevent an affair and a number of marital problems is to learn strong communication skills and use them on a regular, daily basis to maintain contact, interest, excitement, and a good sex life. Good sex without intimacy can lead to affairs just as easily as excellent companionship and emotional intimacy without sex. Beyond that, your character and the commitment you each have to the marriage are the most important deterrents.

Whether one decides to abandon a marriage after an affair is discovered depends on many factors. People often ask if it is possible to recover from an affair. The answer is: Yes! Absolutely!

In my first year as an intern therapist, a couple arrived in my office. Together, they proceeded to tell me that the husband had walked in on his wife having sex with his father. I kept my face perfectly calm, so my eyes wouldn't pop, and carefully repeated what they had said to make sure I had understood correctly. Yep. They then told me, rather matter-of-factly, that his father was "pond scum," or words to that effect, and that he had tricked her. The husband relayed that he had been away a lot and felt partially at fault. They had two children they adored. They talked it over and decided to move 2,000 miles away from his father, to the city where I was learning to be a therapist. They felt they needed a referee to talk about some of the difficult feelings they hadn't talked about, and to save their marriage.

I took a big gulp after listening to this and told them I was unsure and more than a little doubtful that we could save their marriage, but we would certainly try. They came every week for about 12 weeks, and we talked. When they felt they had covered all the issues and we had done a little prevention planning—identifying what signals should bring them back to therapy—I asked them to send me a postcard each year on their anniversary or Christmas. Every year I got a card thanking me, even though I felt I had done nothing. They gave me a great gift: the knowledge that I could never know who would survive an affair and who would not.

> *...and for me to agree to see them in therapy—the spouse having the affair must give up all contact with the affair partner completely.*

Throughout my career, I have had a string of very unlikely couples go on to have much improved and very strong marriages after an affair. In one case, the wife had an abortion with her affair partner, which she confessed to her marital partner. In another instance, both had affairs and decided after many days of talking it over that they were both "trailer trash" and deserved each other. I tell these true stories to my clients so they know that whether they survive an affair has more to do with *them* than with statistics.

I have come to believe that a marriage is more likely to survive when the husband or wife who did not have an affair wants to stay married, feels partially to blame for the problems in the marriage, and wishes to work together to make a better marriage. If they work together to change so that it doesn't happen again, they can succeed. But in order to get on the right track—and for me to agree to see them in therapy—the spouse having the affair must give up all contact with the affair partner completely. I also recommend this partner who had an affair be in individual therapy in addition to couples work. I actually prefer that both partners go to individual therapy. Working this way, we often have success. Often the issues that lead to affairs have more to do with sorting out who you are than changing your partner.

Tips for Preventing and Healing After Affairs

- If you have an affair, see a therapist right away. Many couples survive infidelity.
- Discuss with your partner what he thinks he would do if he or she ever felt like having an affair. Tell him you would like the two of you to talk about it.
- Discuss and set guidelines together about what is appropriate and comfortable with regard to time spent with other people both at work and socially.
- Openly discuss affairs and possible affairs and your comfort with your partner's behavior with people outside the marriage.
- Nothing you can do absolutely guarantees that your partner won't have an affair, so don't worry, make a strong marriage and enjoy the life you have.
- M.A.D. (Make a Date) regularly.

17 Living Happily Together in Tough Economic Times

When my sons were four and six, I received a call at work one day from my architect who had been planning a remodel for us. He told me that my house was sliding down the hill and asked I if could authorize some work. Thus began our first big crisis. Even as I write these words, I feel as stunned as I did then. We wouldn't learn the cause for weeks. (It turns out that a broken, leaking pipe up the hill—that unbeknownst to us, the neighbors had been arguing about whose responsibility it was to fix—was washing away the neighbor's house and taking our backyard and foundation with it.)

I arrived home to a swarm of fire trucks, flashing lights, and lots of yellow "DO NOT CROSS" tape. Three hours later, we had evacuated the contents of our home and gone to stay with friends (for three weeks—and they are still our friends). After that, we lived on the floor of our house for two more weeks with only mattresses for furniture. The reconstruction seemed endless (with cranes and holes through the floors and ceilings) and was still not complete six months later when wildfires broke out and the whole city was swallowed in flames. We were evacuated again. This time our house survived because our architect, an everyday hero, hosed down the roof and wooden decks. I decided remodeling was bad karma and avoided it for ten years.

Because we live in a disaster-prone community, I have seen firsthand the effects of crises on lots of marriages. As a general rule, I recognized that if the marriage was troubled before the crisis, it got significantly worse afterward and often ended. Marriages that were unhappy and had little emotional connection sometimes ended because people decided life was too short to go on like this. In other words, "Who needs this, when times are this tough?"

Happily though, disaster often brought couples closer. Good marriages became stronger. Nearly losing everything made them realize that people matter more than possessions and helped them to appreciate how well they worked as a team. Some crises connected couples to their village of concerned family and friends in a new way that supported their marriage.

Every family faces crises: Heart attacks or death at an early age, death of parents, loss of a home, death of a child, illnesses and, of course, during the recent rapid economic downslide—job losses, foreclosures, and free-falling retirement accounts.

Yet in a general economic downturn everyone together can enjoy the comfort of shared gallows humor, like a friend who wrote: "This recession is worse than a divorce. I lost half my net worth and I still have my spouse!" And you do adjust. You plan less expensive social gatherings and vacations, and enjoy cheap dates together because you and your friends are often in the same boat. And you may feel closer if you risk talking about a subject most forbidden in our society: money! You may spend more time eating at home and talking, and less time going out as a couple or with friends.

There is always a surprise or two in a crisis. For example, one big lesson we learned as a family experiencing a crisis alone, (as opposed to burning in wild fires with a lot of others in your community) is that often it is easier to give than to receive. A friend, who was a big giver in the community, struggled when friends wanted to help him and his family after their house burned down. His friends finally had to sit him down and gently demand that he let them help him and his family. The surprise: our gifts cannot always be received in the spirit we intend to give them. Some people receive with simple surprise and gratitude. Others find gifts as a vote of no confidence or feel like they are being controlled, hemmed in by expectations, and/or uncomfortable about how to respond. Yet, every reaction is valid. Notice how you feel and you will learn about different sensitivities. After a disaster, conversations about time, money, and plans take on a focused, survival quality. There is often much more than ordinary emotional sharing. Many couples comment that they just stop bickering, fighting, or carrying resentments and start talking more—okay, maybe not always in our family, but in many families.

The larger the crisis, the more people want to help. If you need to miss work, everyone understands. Your friends understand if you forget to call. Friends and family spontaneously relieve you of obligations you have assumed. You feel guilt-free eliminating those things you just can't do. A crisis brings the opportunity to rely on each other and people close to you in a new way. Little crises can sometimes be more difficult than large ones. I had lived through fires, floods, landslides, and evacuations, but the most disorganizing of all was when my housekeeper had a complicated birth and took an unexpected eight weeks off in the busiest time of my year. There was no sympathy or community outpouring of support for that. Of course, being a giver, I wasn't great at asking for help either. Our "marital balance" and our personal routines were thrown completely out of whack. Couple time dropped to zero. In these situations, you and your partner need to take quick action together to focus on getting done what is important and letting go of what's not—and maybe asking for help.

Of course, our list of crises also included sudden job losses, income cuts, and abrupt drops in stock prices. In the recent recession, I noticed that we had become old hands at crises. We began working together almost immediately. Here are some working guidelines and hints to take you through a crisis.

Significant crises can also be triggered by or cause small or large traumas. Traumas are encoded in your nervous system in a special way that makes them harder to resolve.

At this point, I will try to take you through a brief overview of the crisis and trauma process.

You may first need a break to pull yourself together and assess your immediate practical needs and your immediate emotional reactions to the crisis. If you can take three to five days to recover, you can then focus on creating a plan of what to do next. You can expect to revise it as you go along. It is best if you can talk about your reactions with someone you trust in this period, log the experience in a journal, or engage in some other form of expression.

Physically, you will have about six to eight weeks where you will act in a state of heightened alertness without starting to have too much physical damage to yourself.

If the stress continues after that, you will normally begin to go into a period of physical letdown and vulnerability to physical illness and mental depression, unless—or even if—you are taking very good care of yourselves. This is the greatest threat period to yourself and your relationships. So it is best to plan for short- and long-term contingencies during the first six weeks.

Everyone Reacts Differently to Crises

No reaction to a trauma or crisis is better than any other. They're just different. As long as you talk about the event fairly quickly, assign some meaning, and take some action every day, you are likely to bounce back regardless of your initial reaction. Those who remain hysterical, in shock, or deny that anything happened, have much greater difficulty in the long run. My husband doesn't like to talk about emergencies. I like to talk a lot! I have learned that if I approach him with specific questions one at a time I get great feedback and it keeps me centered. When I need to vent I talk to girlfriends, write in my journal, or ask for time to vent on our next couple walk. Some Native American tribes have a great ritual: the community surrounds the member in a community circle and lets the member go over their trauma in complete detail, giving full support. Then they are done listening and it is time to get down to action. If you keep repeating the same story more than three times, especially to the same person, you might think about what is keeping you stuck and seek help to begin moving forward. This doesn't mean that you will be completely done reacting after three repetitions, but you can feel your feelings and perceptions beginning to shift.

Knowing your style in a crisis and your spouse's, plus what soothes and focuses each of you, is helpful in handling the steps ahead. Remember, people just respond differently. All the ways they do respond are normal, there is no "right" way.

Some people cry hysterically, some repeat the story of their crisis many times until someone validates the feelings that they can't quite get into words. Some feel rejected and misunderstood and stop talking. Others simply are struck numb, quiet and unmotivated and can't talk at all. Some respond with calm rationality and remain very calm until they are alone with someone they trust, at which time they may burst into tears. Others cry each time they think about it. Some people fly into action to take their minds off the pain. Others may react urgently and impulsively, doing whatever they think might relieve their feelings.

Some people need a plan in order to feel contained before they can express their emotions. Many people can slip into depression and/or shock and become unable to concentrate on the tasks that might help them recover.

Regardless of the initial reaction, anyone may have difficulty reading the materials, forms, and so forth necessary to their recovery and may need help, especially if the depression and/or lack of concentration lasts more than three or four days.

All these reactions are normal and require different coping strategies.

Coping Strategies

Many of us know how to make ourselves feel better when we are upset or down. We each have different means of self-soothing. People's methods often surprise me. Once you become aware of what is most effective for you to soothe yourself, you will often notice that it may not be the same for your partner. Recognizing that you each self-soothe differently and creating space in the marriage for each of your preferred methods will help you both recover faster. Although books have been written on this subject, here are some of the effective methods:

Movement of any kind, such as swimming, biking, walking, running, and jogging helps resolve crises or trauma—especially if you do your talking, thinking, and venting while doing any of these.

Expressing feelings, talking to someone about your feelings about the crisis, helps if you are not forced to do so. Some misguided helpers will try to force you to talk with them immediately. Talking helps only if you want to talk and you trust the person. Repeatedly going over the story to seek sympathy is not so helpful and may drive away your sympathetic listeners. It may also be a symptom of greater difficulties, as I discussed above. Talking about your feelings to gain perspective and a new way of looking at what happened does help.

Reestablishing your comforting routines helps. Anything that you did for fun or social diversion, such as date night and picnics or routine religious and social gatherings can help, even if you skipped them for a few days in the beginning. Journaling, sketching, or coloring is comforting for some people. Others, like me, read self-help and motivational books to get my negative and defeating self-talk back on a more positive track.

Avoid blame. Some people blame themselves when something goes wrong. I was venting to a dear friend after the house slide about some financial outrage or another when she turned to me and said, "You must be being tested for something big." It was the opposite of believing that I was being punished for something awful I had done. It made me laugh—and changed my outlook.

Others blame their partner. Neither leads to a happy ending. I recommend a book called *Radical Forgiveness* by Colin Tipping if you need to work on your blaming.

Be Cautious. Drinking alcohol and overuse of drugs will multiply your problems. But if you do have addiction problems, remind your doctor about this before accepting any medications, because they tend to forget. Eating or sleeping, to excess or too little, can signal that you are having trouble resolving the crisis. Avoid driving when you can and drive very cautiously, because even if you don't drink, you are accident prone for many weeks after a trauma. Meditate and talk with people close to you before you make decisions. You may not be making your best decisions in the middle of a crisis if you act too quickly.

Seek the Lesson and the Gift. Take time to consider your passions and your happiness. I know many people who have lost a job and later find themselves grateful to the person who fired them because they started on a much better path to a job they loved. Affirmations and expressions of gratitude for any tiny little thing can lead to new opportunities. Whining, not so much.

Stick to Good Habits and Principles. In the panic of a financial or emotional crisis, it is easy to rush around ignoring your usual daily routines. This can be liberating at first. And people will support you. One thing I have noticed is that people's crises resolve much more easily if they stick close to what was good in their lives before. If they had a ritual of a special time as a couple or special family time, they kept it, even if they did something free. If they had habits of gratitude, they kept them. People who prayed pray again. People who meditated meditate. If they gave 10 percent of their income to charity and suddenly had no income, they did better if they volunteered a little time to help others. If they always spent less than they made, they modified their budget to keep spending a bit less than they made. If they went into savings, they did so with a plan. People with good habits and good principles recover faster. In general, couples who assess what felt good in the past and stick with it fare better.

Look for the Gift. Once you have addressed the immediate emergency, it helps to look at the gifts that come with a trauma. Initially this may be difficult, but gradually, if you look, you will see. When a quarter of the house foundation slid down the hill, our house was suddenly worth zero, and we had a huge loan to pay. Slowly our financial crisis allowed me to see that I had been way overspending on the kids and probably spoiling them. I began looking into research on money and kids and eventually found *How Much Is Enough?*, a wonderful book by Jean Illsley Clarke, Connie Dawson and David Bredehoft, that tells how to avoid overindulging your kids financially, emotionally, and otherwise. Caution: there are other books with similar names. This one is the best for kids.

Because I held steadfastly to the idea that insurance would make us whole financially (it didn't), we kept spending as we had always done, making our debt greater. By the next crisis, we had learned. We stopped all spending that we could, immediately, and I learned to enjoy all the free time I had when I wasn't shopping. I began to appreciate everything my mom, who grew up in the Depression, had tried to teach me, all of which is now very cool since the green movement became popular. I also noticed how financially conservative friends whose incomes had also been devastated in the recession survived most comfortably because they had little debt and a ready stash of cash, in CDs or bank accounts. I was pleased to be a good model for my kids.

Learn Meditation. Or, return to your meditation practice. I also noticed that in a crisis most people were focused, intense, and worried but not happy. Yet I had known people with severe disabilities and much greater losses who had much better attitudes than mine. Clearly I was missing the point. While many people consider meditation a little mystical or quasi-religious, in fact it is one of the most researched and recommended treatments for anxiety and stress. I decided to explore that. Besides, it's free. I found I needed some guided help to learn meditation. There are many free meditation sites online. My favorite site is the Insight Meditation Center where there are many free talks and meditations to download or to play. An online search for free minute mindfulness meditations produces videos to watch and downloads for an iphone. You can also buy audio CDs and downloads of famous tapes by people such as Jon Kabat-Zinn or (and I love this title) "Full Catastrophe Living." Dr. Kabat-Zinn's program is based on his acclaimed research in the Stress Reduction Clinic at the University of Massachusetts Medical Center. For those with religious faith, there are also Christian and other religious meditation centers listed online. What I discovered as I began practicing meditation, especially a type called lovingkindness meditation, is that I began to experience moments of being happy for no particular reason. I asked my meditating friends and they also noticed it. Studies of people who meditate show that they activate a center of their brain that promotes happiness.

Gain Resilience. I became curious about people who seemed to be happy for no good reason. I had always been aware of a few people like this and they had always seemed vaguely out of touch to me. Didn't they see the real problems surrounding them? Did they live in denial and constantly bump into reality? But as I thought about it, research showed that happy people weren't as accurate as depressed people about facts they were told in a research setting, but they were happier. And people grow richer. I knew from previous research that people making over the median income (or $12,000 at the time, more like $50,000 with current inflation), and even people who are extremely wealthy, are not happier when they have more money, but that happy people grow richer and happier over their lifetimes. I remember a very financially successful comedienne once saying that what she found out when she had lots of money, after growing up poor, is that you're the same as you were before. In other words, if you were a witch before, you become a witch with money. Ironically, while money doesn't buy happiness, happiness begets good fortune. Wild, huh? It seemed to me that logically, happy people had a better deal. They were, well, happier, pretty much without regard for their circumstances.

Imagine my delight when I discovered that Marci Shimoff had written a book called *Happy for No Reason* that summarizes much of the research and literature and has some great stories about people who became happy for no reason. Both the book and CD directions have a happiness workbook, which is downloadable free at her website after you buy the book or CD. From my reading I knew that happiness was about 50 percent genetically inherited and about 50 percent learned. What is exciting about Marci's book is that she explains many practical methods for increasing your happiness set point (or the level of happiness that you return to even if you win the lottery or lose a spouse, like a weight set point), even if you are not genetically gifted with unusual happiness. Many of her exercises are founded in the positive psychology research, others come from experiential techniques. Gretchen Rubin, in her engaging, delightful book, *The Happiness Project*, chronicles her experience with trying various methods for increasing her own happiness. She includes many candid responses from people commenting on her blog about their experiences with various efforts of their own.

Learn Affirmations. When we were in the middle of another financial crisis, I needed help with practical financial guidelines and strategies. I read several interesting books but none were truly practical or inspiring until I discovered *The Wealthy Spirit*. Chellie Campbell had actually lived through a financial disaster. She understood both the financial practicalities and the emotional aspects. She's also funny and upbeat—and she really knew how to use affirmations.

Affirmations are amazing. I had known about using them to help clients. I also learned about redirecting my thoughts. But Chellie had 365 daily meditations for financial well-being linked to short, funny anecdotes. I had to laugh because most of my own self-talk around money was exactly the opposite of positive affirmations. I read it and reread it. She has the most concise description of how to create your personal affirmations I had ever seen, so I began to counter my worst self-talk with short, simple, positive present-tense new affirmations.

Gradually my old depressing thoughts about money and myself started to just drop out of my thoughts. I began to put little nuggets of her wisdom in my phone memo pad. I tried to read and revise them, but most importantly to repeat them. I promised myself to read them when I had to wait in line and before emails, TV, and casual reading. If an affirmation didn't feel absolutely genuine, like *"My clients praise me and pay me."* I would revise it with the word *"can,"* as in, *"I can write a book"* until *"I am writing a book"* felt better.

Express Gratitude. This can be hard! Especially in the beginning when well-meaning people say things like: "Yes, you lost your child, but you have two more!" Ugh. "Yes, you lost your house to foreclosure, but you have not lost a leg." Groan. When people in crisis are treated to these kinds of comments, the comments seem just plain insensitive. And yes, they are. So how do you get to a place where you can express gratitude in the midst of calamity? Although there are many theories about this, I think the simplest way to explain it is to start at the bottom with the smallest thing that you can be grateful for. One couple in the deepest depression decided to meet each night and express gratitude for one thing in their lives. With a lost job and a recent loss of a child, they were feeling hopeless. Finally, the wife, casting about for something to say, said she was grateful for the warm weather. Each night they tried to tell each other one tiny but genuine thing. One night the husband started singing a song and the wife found herself joining him. They started singing together each night and gradually found more and more in their lives to express gratitude. This turned into a habit of singing together that they still treasure.

If you do your affirmations and express genuine gratitude, funny little moments of happiness and gratitude appear. Sometimes, at first, it doesn't feel like gratitude, but if you keep repeating small gratitude statements, the gratitude will begin to feel real. For example, I am genuinely grateful that the crises that befell us and our friends and my clients have taught me so much about trauma and how people deal with it.

Refocus or Set Goals. Initially this may seem too hard. However, a longer time frame stabilizes the present. Some people set goals from the standpoint of what gives meaning to their lives.

Others set financial goals. If you view a financial crisis in the context of your larger love and life goals, it helps shrink it down to size and into perspective so that you can manage it. People who view finances in terms of the seven lean years and the seven rich years of the Old Testament have greater perspective when trouble hits. I talk about how to set goals in Chapter 10.

Seek Outside Help. Help can be assistance with filing forms regarding a catastrophe, advice about taxes, or emotional help. Recognize that you may be more prone to feeling blocked and confused. If you are stuck in a repetitive reaction of any kind—not talking, not eating or any of the symptoms described above—for more than six weeks, seek the help of an experienced and highly recommended trauma counselor. You may benefit from Eye Movement Desensitization and Reprocessing (EMDR), which is the most well-researched trauma treatment and allows people to resolve these issues fairly rapidly. You may also benefit from a crisis group with a therapist trained in short-term crisis recovery methods, especially if your partner and family hate talking about what happened. Research suggests that people who join a group or seek help get jobs faster and build their businesses faster. Good groups for you may not be therapy groups.

Trauma Triggers Can Make Crises Linger

A trauma trigger is an event that vividly brings up the emotions and memories of an earlier crisis. Six months after our landslide, I ran into a trauma trigger. I walked into a house that had been remodeled in exactly the same style as we had been planning for ours. Our house was in post-reconstruction shambles, all our money for our planned decorating and remodeling gone. This triggered a wave of regret.

Although I had been calm and practical during the months of reconstruction, that day I came home, crawled into bed and pulled the covers over my head. I greatly appreciated that when I told Neil what had upset me, he took the kids out for the afternoon so I could cry, sleep, and recover. Even though Neil didn't share my particular upset, he cared that I was hurting and respected my need to deal with my feelings then. Do not be surprised when trauma reactions pop up weeks, months, or years later. Severe grief and trauma reactions return in waves. Depending on the severity of your reaction, you may need to resolve it more quickly or you may want to ride it out. Part of your plan may involve helping your children or close family and friends deal with the crisis.

Children React to Crises in Many Different Ways

The most common reaction is fear. Parent's reactions make a great difference in their child's recovery from disasters and crises.

Stay calm. When parents are calm, their kids are calm. This can keep a crisis from turning into a trauma for them. When parents are agitated and talk about how awful it is, the kids get more worried. Children are most fearful when they don't understand what is happening around them.

Talk to your kids about both the facts and feelings surrounding what happened, in words they understand. My friend Ginger, who was diagnosed with breast cancer and had a double mastectomy, talked to Eve, her three-year-old, about the booboos in her breasts. "I don't really feel bad at all. My booboo is deep inside my breast, so deep that you can't see it. It's called cancer."

As the events unfolded and friends arrived to help, she explained things to Eve. She didn't overload Eve with details she couldn't understand. "Will you be different when you come home?" asked Eve. "Not really," Ginger said. "But my breasts will be different, and I won't be able to hold you like this for a while. I might be very tired, but I'll still be able to love you and kiss you and tuck you into bed at night."

Get their view of the disaster. Children's perspectives are often unique. Children's drawings, especially when they tell you about them, are a window into their special world. After the landslide, I explained to the kids that our house was broken and would need to be fixed. When I explained we would have to stay over at his friend's house, Clark, then five, objected. After a long day at his friend's, he said, "I am ready to go home now and play with my toys." When I explained that they had been packed on big trucks like when we moved, my other son, Xander, then three, said, "You remember moving, Clark—boxes, boxes, boxes!" Clark decided we were better off at Matthew's where the toys were already handy.

In addition to helping make sense of what is happening in their terms there are several steps to help them feel safe.

Reestablish family routines as soon as possible, like stories at bedtime, Saturday mornings with Dad, whatever is comfortable, enjoyable, and familiar.

Allow a little extra time with them. These family rituals help cushion the shock of the disruption. The extra time gives them a chance to talk about their perceptions and fears.

Acknowledge your children's feelings. I told the kids, "Dad and I miss staying at the house, too. But work crews will be there early in the morning to fix the house, and I think they will wake us up."

Try not to spill your anxieties on your children. We didn't talk in front of our children about our concern that the house would continue down the hill, which would have left us homeless. Neil let me get up at 5 a.m. each morning while he stayed with the kids so I could check the progress and relieve my anxieties that the house was still standing, without risk of scaring the kids.

Encourage kids to deal with their feelings through play. Given play materials like family figurines, blocks, toy houses, and fire engines, children will often repeat the same play activity over and over to resolve their emotional feelings. Ginger let Eve participate after Mom's surgery by playing doctor, taking Mom's temperature, putting Band-Aids on her booboos, and playing nurse by rubbing Mom's feet over and over.

Assure them often that they are safe. "I don't think it is safe to be in a broken house right now, but we will be safe there when it is fixed," we told our kids. Be patient. With this, as in all things, children may ask repeatedly for more information about what happened. Avoid giving them too much information. A short, but true answer satisfies them. Repeating the answer when they ask again is reassuring.

Help kids develop a sense of control by participating in activities. After we spent three weeks at friends', we talked to the kids about how it would feel to move back and camp in our house even though it meant sleeping on the living room floor for two weeks until the house was restored enough for our furniture to come back.

Plan on spending extra time with your kids. They will need it. If you can't do it all, friends may help. Eve had Aunt Susie and Godmother Ellen to stay over while Mom had surgery and for the first days of recovery, allowing Daddy to spend more time with Mom.

Plan on needing extra time as a couple, too. Our dear friends swooped down from 40 miles away and offered to take the kids overnight while we evacuated the contents of the house and discussed our options. They were close friends with nice kids, and so our kids happily went off with them even though the house was covered in yellow tape, everything was in boxes, and there were fire trucks everywhere.

Many children begin sleeping with their parents again after a disaster. This is comforting and fun, but eventually needs to end to give the couple private space again. Help children gradually return to their own sleeping space. You may need a mini-step method. For example, they move from the parent's bed to a cot or a sleeping bag in the parent's room. Consider celebrating the return to the child's own room with a special treat like a special dinner or activity.

Avoid being Mr./Ms. Grouch. Frequently a crisis will cause adults to be irritable and grouchy. Try to avoid doing this in front of the kids and, if you do, talk about it, saying something like "I sure am using a grouchy voice. I must be worried or upset about.... I am sorry. How about if I start over?" Then redo your comment nicely, like: "What I meant to say is, I am worried about...and I would really appreciate it if you would help by picking up stuff with me so we can have dinner." Kids need to know that just because you are grumpy you aren't going to leave them or each other or become mean.

Express appreciation. Kids can be little training units. When we express happiness with them and what they do, they respond to adult requests better. If you give positive comments and attention to them at about a five-to-one ratio, they will be quick to respond to your requests and "helpful" training or feedback. If they stop responding, then see paragraph above about Mr. or Ms. Grouch. If you are being positive at a five-to-one ratio and they are still being difficult, they probably need attention or a chance to talk about negative feelings.

Give attention, not money. When you have less money and it feels like you have less time to give, focus your attention intently on your kids and plan time with them so all your energy doesn't go into the crisis. This focused time can become memories that last far longer than anything material.

Expect regression. In crises, kids often retreat to old, outgrown habits of six months ago or longer. They may be potty trained and start having accidents. Nightmares, lack of interest in usual activities, extreme withdrawal, temper outbursts, inability to concentrate, thumb-sucking, bad dreams, fright fantasies, hair pulling or twisting, crying, clinginess, unusual inattentiveness to parent requests and other behaviors of concern are common reactions. If these persist more than four or five weeks, contact your doctor or a counselor trained in trauma with kids. Do not blame your spouse for these problems (well, maybe it feels like better-them-than-you, but no).

The good news is that kids are resilient. Even a small amount of group therapy or EMDR, a trauma therapy mentioned earlier, modified for kids, can help resolve the crisis more quickly. You and your spouse will fare better if you work together as a team to understand what the kids need and make sure they are with people they trust, like one of you, as much as possible. Although people in crisis have a tendency to dwell on their problems, dwell on what you have instead. Express gratitude daily to each other and to your kids. You will be glad you did long after the crisis is resolved.

In short, a crisis is a great opportunity to let go of the negativity and petty frustrations of your old life and create new habits that will help you and yours all for your present and future life. Focus on what you have now and not what you have lost, and you will emerge stronger. Living through tough times can lead to the best and happiest part of your life.

Action Steps in Tough Times

Here are some action steps to take today (not tomorrow— leave that to Scarlett O'Hara).

- Accept that you are upset.
- Regardless of your loss, list things that keep this from being the end of the world.
- Learn to use affirmations.
- Express gratitude daily. Start small.
- Take a good look at your budget within the first two weeks, especially in a financial crisis.
- If you can't give money, give time. Volunteering is healthy.
- Keep up your good habits.
- Learn how to graciously receive help.
- Read stories like Jeanette Walls' *The Glass Castle* about people with exceptionally difficult lives. Or read your favorite escape literature.
- Talk to professionals and people who have been through this kind of crisis.
- Cut expenses and stop buying anything that you can; it is not a good time for "shopping" therapy.

- Be extremely cautious when you drive. Statistically, you are extremely accident-prone in this distracted state. If friends offer to drive, let them.
- Avoid drinking and, for your sake, don't start smoking again. These old habits may seem to reduce stress but, even if you and your partner do them together, they are a source of stress. If you do drink together more than usual, who will watch the kids? Drinking also makes concentrating and making good decisions more difficult.
- Use new prescription anti-depressants and anti-anxiety drugs cautiously and as a last resort because they likewise can affect your judgment, especially when you are just starting them.
- Divide the labor but make many decisions jointly.
- Show respect for each other's decisions.
- Respect the differences in each other's emotional resolution to the crisis. One of you will want to talk a lot and may even need a group. The other may need to meditate more.
- Focus on what you have, not on what you have lost, repeatedly.
- Find whatever positive lessons you can in the experience and share them with each other.
- Seek balance. Eliminate anything that isn't useful, beautiful and joyful in your life!
- Stay focused on good practice.
- Hug a lot.

Part Four

Let's Talk:
Protecting Your Marriage

18 Healed by Listening

Most of us believe that we are pretty good listeners. If the topic is positive and about us, or about our beautiful child, then what we hear is probably pretty accurate. If talk is negative about someone we don't like, we may find it funny. But when negative news about us—or our darling children—reaches our ears, few of us retain a sense of humor or an ability to listen.

"I love you, but I am not in love with you."

"I don't think you have ever really loved me."

"I can't imagine having sex with you ever again."

"Why don't you ever do anything around here?"

"Don't you care about our kids?"

"Don't you care about me?"

"I don't respect your work anymore."

"I don't trust you."

"What kind of father (or mother) would do such a thing?"

These are all things I have heard loving partners say that were hard for their partners to hear. Yet really listening to their partner opened a discussion that made the marriage better.

Most people aren't good listeners in a crisis, because they focus, quite appropriately, on the tasks at hand. Since having kids is a multi-year crisis for most marriages, developing and using your listening skills can work magic in your marriage. Practicing these skills helps you and your partner feel closer. Your multi-year crisis may become a healing crisis, making your marriage stronger than ever.

For good marriages to thrive, each partner needs to be able to express feelings of discomfort, distress and dissatisfaction, and be heard. This doesn't mean anyone needs to tolerate, nor should they spew, a torrent of abuse. Indeed, many women marry with the idea that their partner is a sanctuary where they can share negative feelings. Women often see themselves as a sanctuary for their partners to express vulnerability as well. Most men didn't read that notion in the fine print of their marital contract. Most men find the idea of sharing negative feelings scary, perhaps a little crazy and sometimes unmanly. Men see a good marriage as one where no one needs to talk about problems. But in happy, long-term marriages men and women learn to listen even when what their partner says is negative and about them.

In a marriage with kids, it is common for parents to complain about needing more help or not having the energy for sex. Sometimes, sadly, the complaints fall on deaf ears. Yet if partners learn to listen to each other and try to understand the other partner, sharing with someone who deeply cares about you and working out problems becomes a healing experience—a healing listening for each partner and the marriage. Even better, if you learn to check in regularly with your partner, the negative messages will become less frequent and easier to hear.

BABY BLUES By Rick Kirkman and Jerry Scott

So how do we overcome our natural resistance to hearing something that we don't particularly want to hear? How do we listen in a way that is healing to our partner and healthy for our relationship?

Steps for Difficult Conversations

Step 1: Let the person know you are listening intently. This does not mean you agree with what is being said. This means giving direct eye contact and doing nothing else while they are talking—that includes clicking the remote or watching a muted TV. Look riveted with attention. Sit still and quiet. Nod your head gently and slowly. If the person is saying, "You act like such a jerk sometimes!" nodding your head slowly may seem inappropriate or insincere, but do it anyway. Your rapt attention will be rewarded. Your instinct will be to respond, deflect, or interrupt. If you really can't sit still and listen, grab a big yellow pad and write down each point and reflect later. Here's a *don't*: If the phone, a waiter, or a child tries to interrupt, don't let them. Use the moment to pointedly and gently refocus on your partner's comments.

      Step 2: Repeat back what the person is saying as accurately as you can. If the person is really angry, repeat it word for word. Otherwise, repeat back the central feelings that you are hearing. That big yellow pad comes in handy here. When someone says you are a jerk it will have an amazing impact if you say back, "So you think I am a jerk?" What you may realize is that while you heard, "You are a jerk!" The person may in fact have said, "When will you ever change diapers!" By repeating the words and feelings back, you will discover whether you actually heard what was said. This is enormously important for many women and men. Repeating gives your partner the chance to soften what they said for a better start-up. They may even come up with a more positive statement like, "I wish you would change J's diaper right now."

      Step 3: Sympathize, reflecting the feelings as accurately as you can. Some people call this approach "Oh, poor baby" or "tea and sympathy." Don't worry. This also does not mean that you agree with what the person is saying. "Oh, you sound like you have had a really long day and you need a break!" helps the other person know you care that he or she feels bad.

That may be all that is required. Even if you think they brought it on themselves or caused the problem (thus being a real jerk, in your opinion), reserve judgment, be sympathetic and wait for the whole story. You will often be pleasantly surprised.

Step 4: Ask, "Is there anything more you want to tell me about this?" or "Do you feel I got the heart of what you are saying?" When you feel that you fully understand what your partner has said and you have done a great job of repeating back and sympathizing with the main point, check to see if you are right by asking. Often they will soften what they are saying or begin to resolve whatever the issue is on their own. What sounded in the first sentence like, "You are a lazy, unreliable jerk!" may change. Miracle of miracles, they may say something like, "I love you to death, but I am just so frustrated with my life right now." Your sensitive questions give your partner a second and a third chance to discover more subtle feelings they haven't recognized, and shift to a calmer, more neutral, or positive place.

Fine Points to Get You Though the Tough Spots

Control your fear that they will never stop talking. If you listen well, they will feel calmer and then it will be easier to problem solve. And if you do very skilled listening, there may be no problem left.

When your partner is upset, just listen. Do not agree or disagree. If you try to agree or disagree, this will cause your partner to escalate intensity, repeat him/herself, and prolong your misery. Remember, it's not about you. Even if they are saying, "You never do anything around here!" it is not about you.

When I first try to teach men active listening, they usually say, "It works great if I just agree with everything she says! But I feel like a wimp and I never get my point across." While full agreement may stop arguments, it breeds resentment. *You* feel resentful if you go along and your *mate* feels resentful if you agree and then don't follow through or do something else entirely. These folks miss the point. *Good listening, not agreement, is a better first step.*

Make sure each of you has a full turn to speak before you propose a solution. You *each* need to feel that you have said all you need to say *before* you try to "solve the problem," especially if you are dealing with a hot issue.

Do not offer solutions unless and until you are asked. Men are famously accused of this, but many women do this as well when they feel attacked or just want to be helpful. I know I am repeating myself here: *Listening is not about you, your thoughts, what you remember about what* really *happened, or your solutions.* Your thoughts and feelings are important later in the process but now they are distractions that will interrupt the listening process and block your partner's expression of feelings and block creative, satisfactory solutions. If you feel you have a great solution, ask your partner if he is ready for your ideas before you chime in.

Stay focused on your partner; don't make it about you. Anything that is about you, including your "very interesting opinions," is a distraction and will either shut the person down or prolong the negative part of the discussion. Your solution is probably brilliant, but that isn't listening. When your partner is upset about an issue, even when your name is in his/her story a lot, remember the issue is his/hers, not yours.

Ask for what you need so you can listen well. Many upset wives speak in long complicated paragraphs with footnotes and examples. One trick that therapists use is to ask a long-winded talker to put a complaint in one sentence. Sometimes I teach guys to ask their wives to "Please, boil down the main idea of what you just said to three sentences or less, so I make sure I have your core point."

Recognize the right times to listen. Notice *when* you and your spouse communicate best and try to arrange those times together regularly. Sometimes healing listening isn't required. When your spouse is asking you to please hand him a diaper, hand him a diaper. Nobody asking or giving directions wants you to reflect their feelings. Listening is hardest to do when someone is upset with you, yet that is the most important time to listen. Good listening really calms and soothes your partner when they are upset.

If your partner is screaming upset and you just can't think, leave a note that you want to talk when both of you are calmer.

When you just can't listen, make a plan to talk later. If you are watching a great game on TV or the baby is screaming, say something like, "This sounds really important and I would like to talk about it when I can really focus on you. Can we talk about this when the baby is asleep?" As one mom said, "When my husband is too crabby, I say, 'We'd better talk about this later.' He doesn't necessarily apologize later, but when we try to talk again I can tell he has regrouped and we do better."

If your partner is screaming upset and you just can't think, leave a note that you want to talk when both of you are calmer. Write in a journal, call a counselor or consult a happily married friend before you talk again, but talk to your spouse as you promised.

Sometimes the rules don't apply. If your partner is drunk, listening is a waste of time. Tell him or her that you will talk tomorrow. Don't waste your breath and threaten your marriage by talking to a drunk person. Snuggle, laugh, flee the scene, or go to bed but don't try to have a talk. The conversation will be so much more productive in the morning.

If you are afraid for your physical safety, leave and then call or have a friend call and say you will contact your spouse when you feel safe to do so. Even if the marriage can't be repaired, your life will be easier if you treat your partner with respect while you take the time you need to get focused.

Listening Tips

- Give full eye contact.
- Repeat back the core of what is being said in neutral words.
- Assume your partner has good intentions even when the words hurt.

- Repeat word for word if the speaker seems upset.
- Wait to be invited: Don't ask questions, agree, or offer opinions until your partner has finished saying everything he has to say on that topic and invites a response from you.

19 Recognizing Kinds of Conversation

Some discussions involve "Change Requests," some involve "Problems," and some are simply "Weather Reports." It may be helpful to learn the difference.

A Change Request is an action item. You are unhappy and you need something to change that involves your partner. You may or may not know the solution, but you do know that something in your life needs improvement.

A Problem, on the other hand, is something you want advice about. A problem is an issue that needs a discussion, some proposed solutions, and a plan of action. Problems may involve the kids, friends, or family, but usually are not directed at your partner.

A bid for sympathy or a Weather Report is when you just need to talk through your feelings. You want to know your partner hears you. You want some sympathy and *maybe* a few gently curious questions to encourage you to share. You do not want questions that direct the conversation to something else. You do not want the other person to take it personally or feel criticized. You don't want them to fix anything. That's a weather report. No action required.

Before starting a discussion, say up front, if you can, whether an issue is a change request, a problem, or a weather report. For example, imagine his family is coming for their annual weeklong visit and you know you felt like a house slave last time they were here. You might sit down or take a walk together before the visit and say, "Last time your parents were here, I felt really exhausted. I wonder if we could plan to make it easier for me and everyone this time?" By the same token, let your partner know if you want advice by saying, "This is a problem. I want advice about this." If it is a weather report, say, "I need some talk time to get my feelings out about something." If your partner doesn't tell you what kind of issue it is, then ask before you give advice.

One complaint or change request a week is enough and a good goal to shoot for. (Even though, as my husband will tell you, I will probably never achieve it!) But one complaint a week is an important guideline if you actually want to encourage listening. People quickly stop listening to someone they feel complains a lot. For the same reason, try to keep bad weather reports or serious venting to only once a week also.

Good weather reports can be any time. Asking for advice— but not giving advice—can be any time as well.

When your spouse offers unsolicited advice, say, "Thanks, honey, but I need more talk time to figure out what feels right for me first." If he says, "Let's hire a housekeeper," don't say, "We can't afford it," because it brings up money issues, which is a distraction and may be a hot button. Instead say, "That is sweet of you, but I am not sure a housekeeper would help what I am feeling. I just need to talk for a minute first." *Unles*s, of course, you want a housekeeper. The point is don't argue. Stay focused on what you need to communicate.

Even when your partner is an inattentive listener, give him or her the benefit of the doubt. When we see the best in people, they often rise to the occasion. Even if their words sting, remember they love you and consider the possibility that they are unskilled at communicating or that they are feeling badly and as a result are expressing themselves poorly.

Some therapists and couples believe that if partners are at different ends of a continuum, the reason they unconsciously got together in the first place was so they could learn from one another. For example, the person afraid to ask admires persistence, or someone comfortable with clutter admires neatness. This goes back to an old business saw that "you can build on strengths but you can only mitigate weaknesses." Don't expect to make someone into something they are not. The trick is to enjoy each other's strengths and to learn to work the issues out between you as partners on a team. This strengthens your marriage while battling it out weakens your bond.

SALLY FORTH By Greg Howard and Craig MacIntosh

Here's an even better trick: *learn to love and laugh at your differences.* Stop focusing on your partner's annoying habits and trying to change them. Instead, look for advantages in their behavior. Clutter bugs are often fun, creative, and spontaneous, for example. Neatniks are often reliable and well organized. Good marriages can use some of both.

> *Learn to love and laugh at your differences. Stop focusing on your partner's annoying habits and trying to change them.*

Basically, teaching your partner active listening is training yourself to talk so your partner wants to listen. Both of you will feel better for it. Active listening heals the listener as well as the speaker. By listening and not jumping in to help, you really hear and feel what your partner feels. When both partners work on being better listeners and better communicators, the combination is powerful. Even the thorniest issues can be worked out in ways that make each partner feel considered, cared for and—most important—heard.

THE POSITIVE GAME

I first started playing the positive game with my kids. We originally called it the "No-Nots" game, but that didn't match the spirit of the game. We have various versions, but the person who can make all comments and requests without using a negative word wins. My son liked to set traps for me. So for example, if Xander says, "Do you want to buy me an ice cream? cream?" I must say, "I prefer that you have ice cream after dinner." Likewise if I want something done, instead of saying, "Why don't you pick up in here?" I must say, "Please start picking up now." In the drop-dead version of the game, the person who uses the first negative loses. Sometimes we play for the most positive points or the lowest negative points during a trip to the store. It is scary how hard it is to use positive words and how quickly you lose points.

I use this with clients who are so discouraged about their marriage that they only have negative talk about what is wrong. I teach them to ask for what they want instead of what they don't want. Instead of saying, "I don't think you find me attractive because we never have sex anymore!" which produces a defensive barrage and no action, I ask them to rephrase it to say exactly what they want, as in, "How can we get some quiet time together to have sex?"

20 Fight Like the Windows Are Open

When couples fight, most partners will say things to one another that they wouldn't dream of saying to anyone else—even to someone they do not like. In the heat of battle, many people feel they are fighting for their survival, and they feel compelled to defend themselves aggressively. Fighting like the windows are open means speaking your piece effectively without hurting your partner or provoking a vicious counter attack. In other words, fight like the neighbors can hear you. When you fight with kids in the house, they are listening. And they learn your good and bad habits, not just about fighting but about everything else, too. When they hear tension in the adults' voices, even infants will burst into tears. As they begin to understand language, toddlers and preschoolers become more sensitive.

Yet, couples need to disagree to be happy. One research study actually correlated a husband's ability to effectively express "disgust" or dissatisfaction with long-term marital happiness. Happy couples need to learn to disagree in a way that *not only* does no harm to their marriage, but is also fun and a little playful. Fighting well is a great gift to both yourselves and your kids, and one worth fighting for.

Almost by definition, when you are fighting, as opposed to discussing or disagreeing, you have lost your mind somewhere along the way. At home, couples break all sorts of communication rules that they wouldn't consider breaking elsewhere. I hope to teach you some ways to gain perspective, prevent senseless and repetitive fights, and perhaps even help you learn to laugh at yourselves as you fight.

Here's how one husband described a common fight with his partner: "My wife is always trying to perfect our relationship and especially me. She says things like… 'I wish you would help me more around here and keep up your end of things. I feel like a maid on the weekends while you play with the kids.' Sometimes I answer sarcastically so she will just drop the whole subject: 'If you were earning a salary as a maid, you'd probably have to do a better job.' It's mean, but I just want to relax sometimes, not always run around cleaning. I would rather do something fun together than discuss our relationship."

Almost everyone recognizes a bad fight. This fight is bad because the wife assumes the problem is her partner's fault. He recognizes the problem but doesn't want to talk about it like this. He responds with something mean to deflect her away from the problem. They manage to break several rules in just a few sentences and end up feeling bad and going nowhere. Good fights and good discussions should strengthen both of you and the marriage.

> *I encourage them to recognize the patterns in their fights...*

Often couple fights have a scripted aspect. They are repetitive, and each of you takes the same roles over and over again. To break up these chronic fights, it helps to step back and figure out what the pattern is. Sometimes a friend or counselor can help you back away and see the part each of you plays in the drama.

Learn your partner's role and your own in most of your fights. Over the years I have given names to these fight roles, which I share with my clients to help them laugh at themselves and gain a different perspective. I encourage them to recognize the patterns or cycles in their fights, and then together we find ways to approach the drama differently. In all these conflict patterns, nothing is ever settled and the same fight is revisited repeatedly. However, there are many opportunities to start over and have a happier ending if couples could see how they are stuck. See if you can recognize any of your fights here.

Lawyers in Love

The first pattern is what I like to call **"Lawyers in Love."** *Civil lawyers* in love are quite calm and cold when they argue, although they can manage to sneer, belittle, and blame. *Litigators in Love* are passionate and dramatic. They cross examine each other and set traps. "Ah ha, see. Gotcha!" Both civil lawyers and litigators are equally miserable, although litigators tend to have more fiery divorces. Sometimes these partners have law degrees, but many articulate, devastating "lawyers in love" function scathingly without any legal training.

There are three simple ways to derail lawyers.

First, recognize that litigators feel five years old inside, helpless and vulnerable. Talk to them gently and sympathetically as you would a worried child, and you will find that all the huff goes out of them.

Second, say, "You look like you need a hug. Come sit here and let's start over." While some lawyers balk at this, most melt.

Third, take a time out and write down your complaint in the same kind but firm words that you might say to a friend. This eliminates the belittling tones that flood your partner emotionally. Making yourself write down a complaint forces you to consider whether it is really important, and not just your way of shooting off a trivial criticism.

The Princess and the Peace Seeker

Another pattern is the **Princess (or the Prince)** and the **Peace Seeker.** The Princess always has a clear idea of what she wants and is used to being attended to. The Peace Seeker, a.k.a. the conflict avoider, wishes to keep the peace. He knows the Princess will stomp her foot if she isn't happy or yell in an embarrassing way, so he tries to maneuver about so she won't be disappointed. Often she complains that he won't communicate. He doesn't communicate because he doesn't want to disappoint her.

She usually requests therapy to learn how to communicate with a partner who retreats...and retreats...and retreats or just ignores her requests and needs. The Peace Seeker often feels like a peon and forgets to come to a scheduled appointment or reports that he has to work at the last minute to avoid unpleasantness (and "therapy appointments"). He often treats her like a Princess because he sees her as especially beautiful or talented or both. Yet he wonders why, if he married the Princess, he hasn't become a King by now. And he resents it. He secretly thinks he should be treated as a king and that she should make as many attempts to soothe and guard his feelings as he does for her. Yet he is constantly subject to her whims and criticized for not meeting her standards or anticipating her needs.

Working with the Peace Seeker: The Peace Seeker has great difficulty saying what he or she wants since the peace keeper is trained to make everyone else happy. Often, he or she complies, but resents it. And then eventually someone explodes. Prevent fights with a Peace Seeker by asking them what they want as often as possible. When they say, "What do you want to do?" don't answer first. Instead, learn to say, "I want to do what my honey really wants to do!" Then mean what you say and follow through, even if it seems like a terrible idea.

Most frequently, the Peace Seeker will answer, "It doesn't matter," while thinking, "You are going to do what you want any way." Or, they'll say: "I don't know. What do you want to do?"...again. If you are trying to change the pattern, you will say, "I want to do something that you are excited about doing." Then, be sure to do it or at least incorporate the ideas you have elicited.

The Prince and a Former Princess

Frequently, the Prince makes a lot of money, and the wife, the former princess, is exceptionally attractive and/or much younger. Together they decide that it will be best if she stays home with the kids. She is used to getting a certain amount of attention for being attractive, vivacious, and competent. Now, she stays home and usually gets considerably less social attention. If she was also previously successful in a career field, she feels even more isolated. He doesn't feel as competitive for her attention as he did when he was wooing her, so he often explains to her that things just aren't that exciting after marriage. He believes they aren't supposed to be that exciting and is puzzled by her complaint, seeing her as irrational. Both want to settle down and be taken care of by the other. He dreams about coming home to an adoring wife who frequently says how much she appreciates how hard he works, and who wants to do little favors for him.

She feels lonely, and as a Former Princess, feels poorly attended by her Prince. He feels poorly cared for and retreats from much contact unless he wants sex, which is an activity she now has no interest in because *by now* she has been chasing a child or children all day. She feels like she has been demoted from princess to scullery maid. He has no idea what she is feeling or why she is so upset because he feels they have an agreement and he is carrying his part out to the letter, by earning money. He may be a very attentive father or a very inattentive one depending on how he sees the original agreement and his role.

She finds his behavior confusing, insensitive, and appalling—*anything but* the partnership and respect that she expected and was used to in their courtship.

At first she may try being sweet, kind, and engaging. However, as a former Princess, she knows how to give orders and how to throw one heck of a fit when she gets fed up with the treatment she is receiving. Even though she loves her kids, she fantasizes about going back to work. She would like to wave her hand airily in her husband's face and say, as he does when problems come up: "I need to go to work now." Then leave *him* to feed the squabbling kids.

The Prince, the Princess, and the Former Princess all have a similar underlying problem. As children, their achievements, whether good looks or good deeds or successes, were more important than their feelings. Active listening, carefully and sympathetically, is extremely healing to them because no one has ever cared how they felt. The best response is a big hug and "Let's start over," followed by lots of attention and concern.

Never give in to a Prince or Princess when they are stomping their foot. Wait until they are calm again. Take time to discuss compromises and possible outcomes in moments of relative peace. Take complaints under advisement and consider them very seriously. Resolving their drama often requires a Prince and the Princess to reconsider the original contract and create a marriage that works for both of them.

One of life's great mysteries is how often our partners can get us to act out the role of the opposite sex parent they had at home. That role may be a **Prince, Peace Maker, Lawyer, Rule Maker** or simply an **Angry One**. By doing whatever they did to protect themselves from a difficult parent, they provoke us to react and act like that parent.

The solution is to remind your partner how different you are from his or her parent. When you find yourself acting like your husband's mother, you know you have played out his fantasy of what he expects a woman will be whether it is the real you or not. Often in these fights, you will have a distinct feeling that this is *NOT* me!

Be curious when your partner is upset. Try to figure out what is happening rather than reacting. Notice when you are about to do something that you told yourself you would never do. Then learn to act in a surprising way that doesn't confirm whatever negative expectation or preconceived role your partner has for you. If he or she expects you to blow up and yell, don't. If he or she expects you not to help, help and then ask him how it feels when you follow through. Eventually your partner will begin to notice the differences between you and the old parent role.

Poor fight scripts are like Greek tragedies where the marriage dies at the end. In your current marital play, the lines of your fights are repeated over and over until the players can anticipate each other's responses perfectly. The actors or partners have stopped listening as soon as the play starts and each has little awareness of how the other actor feels while playing the part.

Good fights are more like improvisational theater. One person is upset and initiates the dialogue. The other listens and helps the skit along, taking their cue from the partner until they reach a thorough understanding of each other's feelings and a workable solution.

Sometimes I ask people to role-play their partner with me so that they can feel what that other person is feeling. I play the upset partner's part in a reasonable, non-blaming way. The upset person feels soothed because I articulate his feelings.

> *... no matter who changes the interaction of their usual script or argument, the other partner responds differently, and the conversation takes a better turn.*

The other person responds differently because I am presenting the partner's story (and feelings) in a way that doesn't feel like an attack. He or she usually turns and says to the other partner, "Is that how you really feel?" The partner nods an emphatic yes, relieved to hear what he is feeling presented in a way that seems reasonable and clear and doesn't upset the listening partner. Then I take the other partner's role and demonstrate that it is reasonable from his point of view, too. Now it is the listening partner's opportunity to feel understood and the first partner's chance to see the argument in a new light.

With that exercise, I demonstrate that *no matter who changes the interaction of their usual script or argument, the other partner responds differently,* and the conversation takes a better turn. In other words, if you change your moves, your partner will change the play and the ending will be different and usually better. Each person feels more understood if they can present what they are feeling in a new way.

REDIRECTING UNHAPPY MARITAL SCRIPTS

Learn to apologize. When you break the rules, apologize quickly and either take a break or move on.

Always make full eye contact. Making eye contact is the way we say, "I am here and I am paying attention to you. I care and you matter to me." It is a grounding mechanism that says we are in the same conversation. Many couples resolve issues simply with good, loving eye contact and without further discussion.

Avoid your partner's hot buttons. One couple was struggling with bitter fights early in their marriage when their therapist asked them to each make a list of their partner's vulnerabilities and hot buttons. They double-checked the list to make sure they had every hot button on the list, and then agreed never to use them again. Now they are very happily married and rarely fight. They attribute their clean fight style to simply avoiding each other's hot buttons.

Attack the problem, not the person. Don't try to change your partner. Remember, this person married you because he thought that you thought he was perfect. Instead of trying to change him or tell him what he should do, invite him to help you solve the problem. When you each start to repeat your positions, say, "Remember, we agree about this, this and this. I am on your team. What can we do together about this problem?"

Use a soft start up, not a harsh one. Think before you speak. Then think again. Researchers have demonstrated that they can predict in the first three minutes of a disagreement whether a couple will have a good resolution. They simply watch whether the couple has a harsh or soft start-up. Either the words or the tone of voice can be harsh. I often ask people to listen to themselves and see if they would speak to a close friend, a boss, a housekeeper, or a child the same way they are talking to their spouse. A gentle start up avoids flooding.

Avoid flooding. Most men become upset and floode well before most women. Many men are overwhelmed annoyed tone of voice. Their hearts pound, and they are flooded with adrenaline. They no longer think clearly. They either want to flee or fight to make a point. Useful problem solving is over before the discussion starts. This means that in an argument, the woman often continues her discussion well past the point where a man is emotionally present and able to comprehend or remember what she is saying. A soft start up, slowing the conversation down to a few sentences at a time and using soft voices or putting a problem in writing dramatically improves understanding and reduces flooding.

Skip the Greek chorus. Don't say that you know several other people who agree with your assessment of your partner's poor behavior.

Give Gifts. Recognize good intentions. In marital requests, consider how different it sounds if you say, *"Our relationship makes me feel so protected and connected; I wish we could find more time together,"* versus *"Why can't you schedule more time at home? Don't you care?"* In role-plays, I often highlight the good intentions of the person I am role-playing and the good intentions of the partner.

Use Truce Triggers. Find a key word that signals, we don't have to have this fight. Some people use a hug, a wink, a word, a phrase, or a funny face. Anything works as long as it is your agreed-upon couple signal.

Ask for what you want instead of describing what you don't want. Saying what you don't want is whining, negative, and saps the other person's energy and motivation to talk to you. If you want to understand this idea better, simply stand, close your eyes, and repeat, *"No, no, no!"* to yourself in your childhood language. Repeat the exercise, saying *"Yes, yes, yes!"* Many people are surprised at how they react inside their body. Often people complaining have never thought about what they do want. I can defuse a situation in a role-play by merely asking the complaining partner what I (as the spouse) could do that would make him feel better. If the response is too vague, I ask him again to say exactly what it is that he wants me to do.

Pick a solution that is positive and countable. When you get around to picking a solution for a problem in your marriage, try to make the solution something that you *do* rather than one you do *not* do. And make it an action that you can count. For example, a goal like "helping more" is hard to count. A countable goal would be if the wife agrees to take the trash out every day. In exchange, the husband could agree to do two diaper changes. If either one falls down on the deal, they owe that job plus another duty, so the problem is not ignored and both partners are involved and accountable.

Check the solution for comfort. Can you each picture yourselves doing what you agreed to do? Does the solution address the problem? If the solution involves, for example, making requests in a different way, check how the new way of asking feels and ask how your partner thinks he or she will respond. After you have a comfortable solution, decide on a trial period of a week or two.

Compromise on unsolvable problems and personal quirks. As most people live together they learn that they react very differently to some issues. Learn to work together in ways that protect each person's vulnerabilities. Ask yourselves if the solution takes both people's quirks and personalities into account.

Pick a time to check in with each other about how it worked. In therapy when couples are working on problems and solutions, the next session is the obvious time to check in. In real life, I encourage people to make a regular time to check in with their partners, and make a point of inquiring how they feel the issues they've discussed are working out. Start each check-in by congratulating yourselves on your successes first.

When I describe it, resolving marital misunderstandings seems like an awfully slow process. It is. But it's time well spent because people generally resolve emotional matters best when they do it slowly. Taking it slowly and thoughtfully helps prevent emotional flooding and breaks the cycle of endless repetitive arguments. And when you go slowly and carefully, you are more likely to reach a true resolution so that you never need to have that fight again.

Often, but not always, couples who come to see a therapist are better at resolving conflicts at work than they are at home. Why? It's because at work they are following the rules of fighting like the windows are open. I have asked couples who come to therapy to fight politely in front of me, and also to audiotape their fights at home and bring them in. I don't plan to listen to the tapes, but I want them to see that if they can be civil at work they can be civil at home, too—and they *will* be if they think someone's listening. Fighting like the windows are open works regardless of how you learn to do it.

Tips for Good Fights
If You have a Complaint, Suggestion or Request:

- Make fun of the problem, not the person.
- Make fun of yourself, but not your partner or your kids.
- Commiserate about the problem together if you can.
- When your partner makes a blooper and looks remorseful, be gracious or say nothing. This can pay big dividends next time.
- 'Fess up to your own part in the problem first.
- Try to talk through some solutions in a quiet moment a little before you anticipate a problem may come up again.
- Choose your problem wisely, no more than one a week if you can. Write the others down for another week.
- Compliment your partner on several sincerely wonderful and amazing attributes before you try to bring up a problem.
- Highlight (exaggerate) all your shared values before addressing the problem.
- Keep it light. Come up with as many silly solutions as serious solutions.
- Ask what your partner thinks is a good solution and what he wants to be responsible for.

If Your Partner Has a Complaint:

- Give full attention and be concerned. Good eye contact and sincere, full attention often help resolve the problem quickly.
- Strive for a curious rather than a frustrated or angry tone.
- Try to reflect the depth and extent of the problem. Restate your partner's feelings and the problem as best you can and as often as necessary. Then ask, "Do I understand completely?"
- Ask, "Is there any more I missed?" or "What is it I am not getting?"
- Ask, "Is there anything else you want to tell me about this?"
- If you think your partner does the same thing he or she is accusing you of, ask him in a sincere, if confused way, how what he does is different from what you do.
- Ask all the possible things he has considered or tried in order to resolve the problem and if there are any other ideas your partner might have to solve the problem.
- Suggest goofy solutions as well as serious solutions only after your partner feels you understand well enough and says he or she is ready to try and look at solutions.
- Check back to see how you are doing in resolving the complaint. You get many, many emotional points for that.

21 Taking Care of Yourself

After the birth of your baby, time for yourself is the first to go. Sometimes the reaction to losing that time comes right away. Other times the awareness comes months or years later. Regardless, when you don't care for yourself frustration and irritability inevitably follow.

As a new parent, allow yourself to be a little sad about the carefree life you left behind. When you can, give yourself a little of what you miss most from your old life. By the same token, celebrate what you like about your new life. Granted, much of what is new in your life you will not be able to control because the baby's needs will dictate what happens. See if you can learn to enjoy not having as much control and being spontaneous. Enjoy using the baby as an excuse not to do something you didn't want to do anyway! (I secretly loved telling people I had to leave a party early because of the kids' babysitter so I could go home, without guilt, pull on my jammies and indulge my desire to be a zombie.)

Giving to a child is easy at first, just as giving to your spouse is easy in the honeymoon phase. But if you don't take care of yourself, you will run out of energy to give to both your partner and your child.

Many women suffer from a Cinderella complex and expect to be rescued with more help as they become more drained. Even if you are married to Prince Charming, he is unlikely to truly understand what you need unless you take the time to discover what you need yourself and tell him. Likewise, many guys work intensely at moneymaking, yet never ask themselves if their own work or life brings them joy. This section is to encourage you to develop habits that protect you both from waking up one day a "stranger in a strange land"—your marriage.

The hardest step is choosing and creating personal time. At first, many moms start by trying to include the baby in their personal time. This isn't really personal time, though it is a testament to female creativity. My friend Pam uses the treadmill while feeding her placid and happy daughter. My friend Nicole delivers meals on wheels with her preschooler with the idea that her child is learning to volunteer.

Another new mom found a videotape that focused on doing yoga with a newborn. After work, another mom curls up for half an hour with each kid so she can recharge and enjoy her kids before plunging into dinner. She feels rested and ready to go, and her kids get some welcomed special time with Mom. These are wonderful activities that recharge both Mom and baby. They reduce the chaos and create a nice routine. The problem is they don't create personal time for the parent.

To feel centered, each parent needs definite alone time set aside with no little person in tow. Neil counted listening to blaring rock music alone in the car as his quality personal time. That wouldn't work for me. Many mothers tell me they find focus time by getting up early or staying up late to be alone in the house on their computer or reading or exercising. This is a workable solution for many but has another significant snag. Sometimes the partner staying up has such a good time, he or she becomes sleep deprived. The other partner often feels avoided and left out if alone time means skipping couple time to cuddle before falling asleep or early in the morning.

Janice's husband would stay up late on the computer rather than coming to bed. She felt that he was avoiding sex with her. Jeff's desire was to become a web designer so he would no longer have to work in an uncreative job. He felt that the late hours were his only chance to create the work life he wanted without threatening their finances. He saw it as extra work he was doing for himself, the family, and his own sanity. When Janice understood his goal, she was able to be more comfortable. They decided to make certain nights his, hers and ours so they could each have private time as well as couple time. Jeff then set an alarm so he wouldn't work too long and be cranky. Another couple solved a similar problem by Dad cuddling with Mom until she fell asleep and then getting up to play on his computer.

Some of your recharge time needs to be energetic, like exercise, and some needs to be quiet or spiritual, like meditating, listening to music, going to church, writing in a journal, or reading inspirational literature or a novel.

Part of self-nurturing for both partners needs to be connecting with people other than your spouse so that your spouse doesn't feel required to meet all your social needs. Socializing with others also makes you a more interesting partner. Sometimes connecting with people can be combined with exercise, like walking with someone, or it could be attending church.

I have a wonderful "bad girls" group. Every two months or so, we meet without kids, dress nicely and eat, drink, and talk all afternoon. That is as "bad" as it gets with kids. I also love walking with my friend Suzy early in the morning while our kids and husbands sleep. We can laugh about the latest nightmare activity we have done as parents, or puzzle about the idiosyncrasies of our spouses or kids.

Make sure that if golf or marathon shopping is your thing, that your partner has as much time as you do for his or her activities, and that whatever you choose doesn't rob from your couple time together.

Depending how this is handled, leaving the kids with your spouse can actually enhance your relationship with each other and your relationship with your kids. As a general guideline, however, it only enhances them up to a point. Too many traveling days away from your kids begins to feel like single parenting to the parent at home, and like visitation rights to the weary traveler.

Many couples with one spouse who travels a lot send the other on a getaway at least once a year so that the one normally at home can experience time away from the kids and the other can experience time alone with kids. The switch in roles gives them greater empathy for each other, and the kids often love the change in routine. As one mom said, "My kids love when Daddy's on duty because he gives them soda. We all know it's okay on his watch, but not on mine. They can handle that we don't always present a united front." Not only can kids handle it, it models flexibility in their parents' relationship. The same mom added, "When I go away, the girls learn that moms don't always stay home. I want them to have a life when they grow up, too!"

If you don't feel safe leaving your kids with your spouse, you may want to consider why this is a problem. Is there a major problem, like drug or alcohol abuse, or is it just that you need to have things done your way? Can your kids be left with anyone else? If you decide the problem is yours and not your spouse's, you will benefit from occasional time away from your kids. Meanwhile, the kids and your spouse will benefit from their special time together. However, if you really can't imagine doing this, you may want to closely consider what you and your partner are each doing to contribute to this lack of trust and find a way to remedy it.

As you can see from my examples, recharging, self-care activities don't have to be wildly original. Anything that you really love to do and that makes you feel recharged works. Use self-nurturing time as an opportunity to carry out some of the exercises I have talked about in the preceding chapters. Reflect on the incredible changes that you and your marriage are experiencing.

Taking care of yourself and feeling content with your priorities and choices are terrific contributions to your partnership. Help your partner get the time he or she needs without forgetting to take the time you need as well. The key questions are: "Do we get the time we need as a couple? Do we each get about the same time alone?" If the answer to both is yes, then you are taking good care of yourselves and each other.

Self Nurturing Tips

- Focus on healthy escapes. Go for a walk alone. Stay in the shower longer. Call a friend regularly to go for walks.
- Pamper yourself while your spouse takes the kids to the park or a movie. Have your hair or nails done. Get together with a friend and do each other's hair and nails. Get a massage. Read a book. Lock yourself in the bathroom, turn up the music and take a bubble bath.
- Center yourself. Meditate. Practice Yoga. Keep a journal.
- Exercise: Dance. Schedule a regular tennis game with a friend.
- Nap.
- Stimulate your creativity. Start a hobby, like quilting, painting, or making scrapbooks for the family.
- Rediscover an old hobby that has nothing to do with the baby.
- Rent a movie.
- Read spiritual books.
- Go to the mountains.
- Take a class and let your husband watch the baby.
- Watch the history channel. (I never do this, but my husband loves it!)
- Go to an art museum alone or with a friend.
- Listen to your favorite music rather than kiddie music.
- Make a romantic meal to eat together when the kids are asleep.
- Get out and do volunteer work.
- Do nothing and don't feel guilty.

22 Protecting Your Marriage with Warmth and Persuasion

The *formula* for taking care of your marriage is fairly simple, but the *execution* when you have young children is difficult. The trick is to establish routines that support your marriage.

John Gottman of the Seattle Love Lab and author of several books about what makes marriages work, says that couples in happy marriages spend about five hours a week doing the following six things:

1. **Say goodbye with eye contact and affection** when your spouse is leaving for work. Make sure you know at least one significant activity that your spouse has to do that day—a meeting, a sales presentation, finishing a chunk of work, a scheduled phone call with a friend, or avoiding an annoying colleague.

2. **Set aside 20 to 30 minutes of your day to check-in** with each other about what is going on in each other's lives. Take turns being the star and brag and/or complain about what is tough. Don't give unsolicited advice. Show genuine interest. Communicate understanding of bad feelings and good. "That's fabulous!" "You must feel so proud of yourself!" Happy couples are good celebrators of each other's successes. They also respond to negative news saying words like "I am so sorry she said that. What in the world makes her think that is okay." Let your partner know that his or her feelings make sense to you. Take your partner's side. See it entirely from your partner's point of view for this time. You can come back and talk about a different angle on it later. Let him/her

know that you are in this together and will support each other, all things you would do for a best friend and more.

3. **Show your happiness** when you see each other at the end of the day. Even if the baby is screaming or you are chasing a toddler around, stop and share a hug, even a group hug. Give that special, "Hey, You!" glad-to-see-you hello that no one else gets.

4. **Hug your partner** or pat them when you walk by. Touch or cuddle when you are reconnecting. If you don't feel up to sex on a given day, do some special stroking or touching so that you feel connected when you do have energy for sex. Make sure you kiss each other before going to bed.

5. **Make a date.** Am I repeating myself? Yes, because it is important. If you need to, plan what you are going to talk about during the date. This may be helpful especially if you are distracted and tired.

6. **Protect the civility of your marriage: don't foul the nest.** Under the stress of raising kids, it is easy to engage in unpleasant and irritable behavior, such as yelling and swearing, that you didn't do before kids. Watch out for those. Couples do better when they have high expectations for civility and eliminate sarcasm, irritability, and meanness when it creeps into the marriage. Although I have encouraged you to lower your expectations about what you can get done in a day now that kids are here, *don't* lower your expectations for how you treat each other. Use signs of anger as a way to detect problems and improve your marriage. Don't let your expectations for treating each other respectfully slide just because you are tired and grouchy.

If you detect a problem, remember the goals for good communication. Use a soft start-up. "Hey, you sound unhappy, honey. What is going on?"

Many a husband or wife in a happy marriage knows when not to be around or not to try to talk. For instance, pilots who fly overnight trips and are sleep deprived may be grumpy when they get home. A smart spouse chooses that time to run errands or take the kids on a play date. Some people aren't fun when they have to meet a deadline: A smart partner takes the kids to visit a friend. Whatever your strategy, work together to make sure that you don't foul the nest with unpleasant words. Join together against an issue or problem.

If you detect a problem, remember the goals for good communication. Use a soft start-up. "Hey, you sound unhappy, honey. What is going on?"

In addition to maintaining a warm home environment, I'd like to talk about the fine art of persuading your spouse. Many people think that persuasion is manipulative. I don't. I think it is a loving act to study your spouse's reactions and learn to present your ideas in a way that works for you both. Trust me; many moms spend hours deciphering the needs and personalities of their babies, and many more hours as they mature to teenagers. If they spent just a bit of time figuring out how to work with their spouse, both partners would be much happier. What is amazing to me is clients can often recite chapter and verse about what doesn't work, but are in a fog about what does work.

In all my years of doing marriage counseling, I cannot think of any couple in which both partners read self-help books and few where both wanted counseling. I assume that one of you will make it to the end of this book and one will not. Most likely, one of you will be more excited and motivated about working on your marriage. The other will see a new idea or suggestion as criticism of the marriage or more likely, and worse, as personal criticism. This will lead to conversations like "Our marriage is just fine. We are closer than most couples I know." Or, "Why do you read that stuff?" The process will quickly derail.

In order for a marriage to succeed, each person needs to be able to influence the partner to participate in plans and ideas that are exciting to them and to halt things that just don't work. To persuade your partner to try any of the tons of specific suggestions I have given you throughout this book so far, here are some ways that may be comfortable for both of you and get good results. You will need to experiment and find the method that actually works for you and your partner, one that feels comfortable for the two of you.

The "Nose-in-the-Tent" Method

Start with one positive comment related to the idea rather than asking for a big change. Over the course of days, add a bit to the idea. For example, if you're a guy who wants to establish a habit of going to the lake together, you go on and on about how great it was when you used to go there just the two of you. After a few days, when this sinks in, then you add how you're afraid that she is such a wonderful mother and community member that the two of you will get too busy to schedule anything together. A few days after that, repeat again how happy you feel every time you think of your time together at the lake. Then add that you were wondering if you could possibly plan a weekend away in a few months, so that you could have something to look forward to and daydream about. Then you might add that planning ahead is great because you would have plenty of time to find a baby sitter, and so forth. The key is to get a commitment to do it one time rather than moving directly to asking for it to be a habit. Eventually, suggest that since it makes you both so happy, maybe you could make it a ritual to plan your next weekend away on your first date night after you return. The point is that if you have a good time and begin planning for the next good time it will more naturally become a habit or ritual.

The "Creating-a-Chief" Method

I once used this approach with astonishing success with Neil. He refused to go over our finances in any way. He always felt he should be making more money although I thought he made plenty. I was feeling overburdened and said I wondered if he would look into how the children's and our family's mutual funds should be invested. I told him he was quite good with numbers. (He is fabulous.) I said he was really good at learning things quickly and applying what he learned so he could probably do a better job than I could. He agreed to take on the job and become chief mutual-fund man in our family. Fortunately, it was just in time. I had everything in aggressive growth funds and he invested some of our money in value stocks just before the tech wreck of late 2000. This was a big ego boost for him, and he has maintained his specialty. As the kids grew older, we started having brief family financial meetings with the kids every six months or so, complete with handouts provided by Dad, to discuss where we were investing and why! I was shocked and thrilled (the boys, not so much).

I was seeing a couple in which the husband really wanted more fun in their marriage. I asked the husband to become the family "funmeister" and kidnap everyone on Saturday mornings. This stopped an ongoing family feud that went, "You aren't any fun anymore" and "I am a fun person and I always have been," and got them moving in a direction that was more satisfying for both of them.

The "Pleasant Surprise" Approach

Let's say that you want to get a regular date night started because you haven't dated in a long time. You check both your calendars, pick a spot, schedule a babysitter, and announce the plan as a pleasant surprise.

If you have never hired a babysitter, you can ask, "Suppose I wanted to surprise you by getting a babysitter so we can go out on a date? Who would I call for advice?" Or, if you know who her best friend is, you can call and ask her to recommend an acceptable babysitter. Or perhaps you can call the last babysitter she used. A simpler solution is to ask your partner to pick a day and get a babysitter and promise to surprise her with the rest of the fun.

The "Trial Balloon" Approach

Bring up an idea *very* tentatively and include some of the reasons why it may not be such a great idea. This works best if your partner always says no to new ideas and if you have the reputation of coming on too strong or too suddenly. "You know sometimes I feel like with all the rushing around we do with kids that we need to sit down and talk together about our goals for our family, our kids and our marriage. But I don't know where we would ever get the time to do it. And you probably wouldn't want to spend a lot of time doing that. It might make you feel antsy." Then you wait (and wait and wait) for your partner to say, "Well, what would you talk about?" Also if you give a small sample of goal setting and have it work out and then fan the flames before going on to bigger plans, like a whole goal-setting weekend, it works better.

My girlfriend, Marcy, had another example that reverses the approach and leads with the positives. She said, "A friend of mine called and invited my family and me for a weekend at a beach house in Mexico. I knew Donny wouldn't go for this because he doesn't like traveling with other families and he doesn't like Mexico. But I wanted to go so I said it like this, "How would you like to spend a free weekend at a great beach house right on the sand. There are only two catches.

"(*Free* works because the main reason we don't go away right now is money.) I didn't mislead because I said there were two hitches up front. But by then I had his interest. Because I presented the good before the bad, he bought it and we went and had a great time."

The point of the method is to pique your partner's curiosity with an idea and mention that you know there might be drawbacks, so he or she doesn't feel forced and doesn't give an immediate no.

The "Fanning-the-Flames" Approach

To pull this one off, it really helps to be a southern belle—which I am not. The strategy involves finding an example of something that you would like more of and carrying on about how fabulous it makes you feel. Let's say that you like positive feedback. So you say, "You know, the other day when you said I looked good before work, it made me happy all day. I told Jane how happy it made me feel. She said how lucky I was to be married to a charmer like you." Then you warmly tell someone else, while he is in earshot, how wonderful he is about compliments. Most people think that this will not work and that the other person will realize you are angling for something. But you would be surprised how many people just love this approach and will do more of whatever it is that made you feel so good that you keep commenting about it. The key is to let your partner experience your enthusiasm and how happy this makes you feel.

The "Raise-the-Issue" Approach

The key to this method is to do so without proposing a specific solution, so your partner has plenty of room to give suggestions. Saying, "I sure miss going out on dates with you" is an example. This will produce a rain of practical objections from some people like, "Where will we get the money? Who can baby-sit? *When* can we do it??" Just listen and say, "I know you are absolutely right but I still wish we could figure out a way."

For some spouses, especially those who might otherwise argue the point into the ground, this will produce action or a suggested solution in a week or so. If a week seems like a long time, I point out to clients that they have a spouse who may have been rushed and forced into activities as a child and who must always say no before saying yes. So I encourage them to ask early and be patient.

Sometimes, though, the suggestions or response will blow your socks off. Let's say that you are looking for more sex or more cuddling and affection. If you say, "I'd like to try some new things sexually to see if we can have more excitement," and your partner might say, "Let's get a porno flick to watch together!" You might be thrilled or you might feel like you got more than you bargained for.

The "Consider the Big Picture" Approach

Bring up the big picture of your relationship and how you would like it to improve. "How are you feeling about our relationship lately?" This is a hard question for men to ask and an easy one for women to ask. Men are always afraid to hear the wrong answer from their partner. Women assume any answer is interesting. But a woman gives a man big points just for asking, whether the woman feels positive or negative at the moment. Obviously, asking the big question about the relationship scores men more points than women. Sometimes, I think men deduct points if you ask this question.

Carefully rehearse the question about the relationship in your mind so the tone is warm or write it out in a note. Set a warm tone by sharing some positive feelings. Without the right friendly tone, the question may sound as though you are threatening to ask for a divorce or asking for such a big change that your partner will feel intimidated and inadequate. If you are angry, this is very hard to pull off well without sounding grinchy, depressed, insecure, and/or critical. Don't tie a general relationship question to any specific change request and especially don't tie it to a change in your partner. Even more importantly, do not link it to a change that you have asked for already and been refused. Done well, though, this is a magical question that invites the partner to talk about what is good and not so good or helps you to explore what makes you feel cared about and not so cared about, which leads to productive conversation.

The "Direct Approach"

Many men will tell you that this is their favorite approach. The key is to keep it short, positive, clear and to the point. Indicate the positive benefits or rationale for the request. A simple suggestion with genuine positive enthusiasm works wonders. "Let's go on a date this Saturday night. I miss you." You can expect there will be minor negotiation like "Will you get the sitter if I pick the place and make a reservation?" Sometimes if you have a good idea your partner just says "sure."

The critical thing is do not say: "We haven't been out in forever" or "Why don't you ever take me out?" Keep it simple, straightforward and positive. I tell clients to look for the word "not" in the sentence. If it is there, rephrase the sentence.

If the person says, "We can't afford it," or "I can't find a babysitter," don't take it personally. Recognize that if the date or whatever you are requesting hasn't happened before, it will probably take more than one request and perhaps an offer to help. Say, "When would be a better time?" Or say, "Can I help by calling so and so to find a sitter?" Or offer to do something really cheap like take a romantic walk and have a picnic. The point is to indicate how much you want your partner's company and treat discouragement as just a step to success.

Try this technique first on simple requests. Before using the technique on something more loaded, see how it works when you want help with a task. I've found that saying, "Would you please take out the trash?" in a pleasant tone without sarcasm works a lot better than: "I can't believe you could continue to walk by this trash can and not take it out!"

These techniques are very different. People who respond to one may be repulsed or irritated by another. Notice your partner's reaction and use the ones that seem most pleasing to him. Regardless of what approach or approaches work for your partner, always use the "Rewarding a Yes!" strategy. In my practice I often see attempts at persuasion sabotaged. Once they have succeeded in getting their partner to say yes, the persuader will say something discouraging like, "He says that here, but it will never happen," or, "Why are you saying 'yes' now when you said 'no' before?" "Why didn't you say that sooner and we probably wouldn't be spending all this money on counseling?" Or my personal favorite: "Yeah, but he doesn't really *want* to. He is just doing it because I asked him to." They have little insight into the fact that their discouraging response stops the action. Then they can't understand why the partner is suddenly unwilling again.

So *if you have a partner who always says "no,"* think what you do when he says "yes." And think about what you say when he says say "no." Ask yourself, "How would I respond to a friend who asked the same thing? How do I respond when I need a friend's help and he says 'yes'?"

If neither of you can really talk about the changes you need in a constructive way, you may need to ask your partner to go to therapy. Obviously you don't say, "You seem so miserable, you need therapy!" Likewise it is better not to say, "I am miserable, you need therapy," (although you would be surprised the number of cases that start this way). Instead say, "I am really unhappy and I would like to find out why. The Joneses, who are really comfortable and happy now in their marriage, say they saw a counselor named Mr. Swift and I would like us to talk to him too." Or say, "I can picture us in a happier marriage, but I don't know how to talk about it to you in a way that doesn't upset you and hurt your feelings. So, I would like us to talk to a counselor about it. Jane and Jacob are really happy. They saw a Dr. Speedy, who really turned things around for them."

If your partner still refuses to go, or isn't ready, then go alone and work with your counselor to change yourself to learn gentle ways that will strengthen you and the marriage.

Every marriage is filled with irresolvable differences. Sometimes they are thermostat wars, like who sleeps with the window open and who sleeps with the window closed. "I love loud rock music!" versus "That hurts my ears!" Most of these issues can be settled with creative compromise like earplugs or headphones or an extra blanket. The compromises are easier if you show concern for your partner. "Well, I don't want your tender ears to hurt, but I need some time to unwind to music. How can we work this out?"

The greatest thing you can do to take care of your marriage is learn to talk about difficult things in a way that doesn't hurt you or your partner. Then build on that by learning to persuade each other in ways that allow you to experiment and try new activities together. Learning this one thing opens the door to a long and happy marriage.

Marriage Care Tips

- Put as much—or more—effort into keeping your conversation clean and supportive as you put into looking good or caring for your kids.
- Remember when you stand your ground about something that being right in an argument is not as important as being warm. Being right and not being warm doesn't get you very far.
- When you are balancing your budget and assessing what you own and what you owe, count how many times you laughed together this week, too.
- When your partner is upset, let her or him know she or he is first priority with you.
- Search for simple things to praise.
- Make happy comments regularly.
- Keep symbols around the house, in the car and at work that remind you of each other. Pictures are great. People also use jewelry, crosses, stones from their hikes, framed children's art at work, and delightfully creative items.
- Use those symbols to remind you to express happiness and gratitude to each other regularly.

23 Happy Endings

Friends of ours sent out a notice for their 25th anniversary celebration listing five years of bliss, five years of fun, five years of doing it all wrong, five years of getting it right, and five years of renewal—not necessarily in that order. Obviously, they know from experience that long marriages are a mix of ups and downs, stages and ages. Understanding how marriages evolve can help you to weather the inevitable rough spots, just like understanding your kids' developmental stages can help you hang onto the boat through the rough seas with them.

As you watch your young children develop, you will see a process unfold that is parallel to the one unfolding in your marriage. If you carefully nurture your marriage in its infancy and formative years, it will sustain you for the rest of your life. The bliss stage is parallel to infancy. The baby can feel no difference between itself and the caregiver.

Eventually, the baby discovers the differences and frustrations of being separate. By two-and-a-half, she says "no" in order to experience the fun of being a different and separate little person. "This is me, and I am not you!" In the same way, partners discover that they are different. Some people are frustrated and angry about these differences.

Hang in there and you may actually enjoy them, just as a good parent enjoys a child's "no" because it is a sign of independence. Meanwhile, the good parent learns to work with the child so tasks that need to get done get done, without spanking, hitting, or spoiling. In a good marriage, the partners each recognize that their differences are a normal part of the development of the marriage and important to their personal growth. They learn to disagree in a way that is no longer dismissive, critical, and hurtful. Sometimes it is playful, idiosyncratic, and fun.

Just as a good parent sees that the child's attempts at independence are not aimed at hurting them, a good partner recognizes that separate interests, tastes, wishes, and desires are not a catastrophe. Acceptance seems to be the biggest stretch that independent people give to each other. The pain and disruption of an affair or flirtation can derail this stage or serve as an unusually difficult place from which to develop acceptance and re-establish connection.

Just as some parents try to raise their children as little replicas of themselves or to fulfill their unfulfilled ambitions, so too do some spouses demand their partners behave in certain expected ways. Some children don't develop their own identities and succumb easily to the influence of their peers in their teens because they haven't made their own decisions or found their own voice with their parents. Some people drop out of a marriage because they are afraid to tell their partners who they are until it is too late.

Good parents are curious about who their kids are and what they feel. Likewise in a good marriage both partners are genuinely curious about how the other feels.

Just as good parents often grieve privately about what they dreamed for their kids but may never be, so couples must give up many a fixed notion of what they imagined would be in the marriage. When I was growing up, my family sat around the dinner table and talked every night. Now, years later, I remember the exact restaurant I was crying in (while Neil was hoping the floor would swallow us) because I realized that our family—with active boys and dual careers—would never exactly repeat the family dinner experience of my childhood in a family of girls and a stay-at-home mom. Yet once I gave up that dream as a demand, Neil began making sure we had more meals with the kids. Now he is more fun at the table because he doesn't feel forced to be there. Some people feel that when this grieving for the dream sets in, the marriage is over. But sometimes the grieving and the letting go of having to have something exactly your way is a first step to a better marriage. That better relationship isn't just you or your partner's fantasy marriage, but a true blending of both your dreams.

> *As the marriage grows, you share empathy and intimacy in a way that you couldn't have imagined or understood while you were in the honeymoon stage.*

By age three, the young child often begins a pattern of play where he/she runs to Mommy or Daddy and hugs a knee and then runs off to play with peers only to return frequently and touch base. Parents enjoy that running and returning pattern because they see that the child is developing an independent sense of self that feels good because of the trust the parent has created in home base. Likewise, in a solid marriage there are times to develop your own identity in your careers and your friendships with other people, and then return to the safety and connection of a good marriage.

As the marriage grows, you share empathy and intimacy in a way that you couldn't have imagined or understood in the honeymoon stage. This is a critical transformation. In a strong marriage, partners are curious about each other's feelings, wishes, and desires. They make time in the marriage to ask these deeper questions and really listen to the answers. The marriage becomes strong and vital as you each begin to see each other as you really are, with a sense of deep acceptance, and encourage each other to develop into the strong, interesting person you each can be. You each enjoy being known and accepted as you are.

Happily married couples intrigue me. I remember a brief conversation I had with a woman after overhearing her cheerfully saying into her cell phone. "Honey, I love you and can't wait to get home so we can talk more." Someone waiting with us commented, "Honeymooners are so great to watch." She laughed and said she had been married ten years and had an eight-year-old daughter.

When I told her about the book I was writing, she told me that after the birth of their child, she and her husband had started fighting. She said that at the time she had complained that he didn't take care of the baby just the way she wanted and that he didn't change diapers enough. She had griped to her friends about not getting enough help and thought about divorce. She told me, "He wouldn't go to counseling, so I went alone at first. I realized that in my desire to be a good mom I had become a crummy wife. I had changed as much or more than my poor husband. I had forgotten that my husband and I needed time together for just the two of us. Eventually he came to counseling with me. We learned that when you give a little, you get a little and when you give a lot, you get a lot."

She inspired me, and it struck me at the time that many happily married couples had reported a rough spot a few years after the baby was born and a brief period of counseling before their marriages got back on track. I came away from our discussion with a renewed faith in the resilience of people and marriages. In our brief conversation, she had described moving through the five stages of marriage to a very happy, grateful place.

In a good marriage with kids, people change often. Learning how to change and support each other's changes are the biggest tasks you face. Succeeding at learning to change gracefully sets the stage for a long and happy married life.

Good marriage habits are a protective shield around the family. That shield allows them to weather change and accept differences with as little stress as possible. They can then spend more time enjoying one another.

Above all, remember, during the kid crisis in your marriage, you will experience moments, days—even weeks, months or years—when you wonder why you ever thought that marrying this partner and having kids was a good idea. The trouble is normal and the effort to fix it is well worth the time, energy, and commitment. People who achieve a long, satisfying marriage with children gain what is possibly the most personally enriching, fulfilling experience we can have in this life. What could be more important than creating an enduring, healthy relationship that your children will carry on to future generations? When the going gets tough, I hope you will think back to this little book and find some words to inspire you to be kinder and gentler, more curious about each other, and ultimately to have more fun.

Remember, celebrate your marriage as much as you celebrate your kids.

Tips for Enjoying Your Marriage with Kids

- When you are moving from a life of movies and dinner out to a life of takeout and videos, take time to make eye contact and kiss.
- When she leaves her purse on top of the car and drives away because she was strapping the baby in the car, laugh; don't lecture.
- Count those battle scars on the furniture as tributes to a relaxed Mom or Dad. This says, "You are more important to me than stains on the furniture."
- Focus on what a thorough job she does packing for a picnic, rather than how she slows things down.
- Accept apologies.
- Strive to fully understand injuries.
- Learn to take "do overs" when either of you need them.
- Ask for breaks when you need them.
- Calm yourself down before you load and fire with your mouth.
- Recognize that most of the time your partner has good intentions or is clueless. He or she is rarely out to get you.
- After an argument, comment on how well you work things out and how good other aspects of the marriage are.
- Schedule fun and downtime into every day.
- Find fun and different ways to say "I love you" to your partner each and every day.
- Tell your partner often that you are proud of him.
- Celebrate your marriage as much as you celebrate your kids.

Acknowledgments

This book is a love note to my husband, Neil, who never read a whole self-help book in his life until this one. He skillfully guards the happiness of our marriage, puts up with my experiments, and helps me laugh at myself.

My fear is that I will forget to thank someone because so many people have helped me along the way. Ira Poll, the best, most fabulous, and most fun therapist I know, believed in this project when it was just an idea. A warm friend, she made me read the first pages aloud and provided encouragement, endless inspiration, great stories, gentle critiques and laughter.

Special thanks also go to my friend—writer, humorist and newspaper columnist Marni Jameson—a mother of two who brought both her professional touch and her mothering experiences to the whole manuscript. I loved that she has girls and so a very different experience from mine. She and her husband, Dan, helped me carry it over the deadline to the finish line and encouraged me when I needed it most. She coaches, teaches, and empowers. She also suggested the tips, so I nicknamed her "Mother of the Tips."

Deborah Allen, another wonderful therapist, read every word and contributed many perfect phrases and experiences. She is a funny lady and should write her own book.

Two terrific dads and very fine husbands, Doug Anderson and Neil Poll, read chapter after chapter on the computer and gave me detailed feedback—catching me when I wasn't clear or didn't speak to the male ear.

My sisters—Allyn Kahle, Gay Ummel, and Larke Recchie—are all wonderful moms. Each had the wisdom to marry excellent husbands and good fathers. Jim Kahle and Ron

Meiloch read early drafts and provided encouragement. Our parents, Clark and Carolyn Ummel, gave us everything that we needed.

Besides Ira, my other sisters of choice, the Bad Girl Judy Anderson, Linda Bennett and Lucyann Carlton—great moms and therapists all—read early drafts and provided unstinting encouragement. Suzy Willhoit, queen of "fight like the windows are open" marched up and down the hills with me on our daily walks listening to my writer's quandaries. Two other good therapists, Geoff White and Michelle Massey, supported my writing. Jeanne Reiss, Larna Scholl, and Sari Poll supported my life so that I had time to write.

My New York partner, Ellen McGrath—a great coach, author, and therapist—continues to make important contributions to the field. Her experience as an author gave me the courage to start my own book. She is my coaching buddy.

My agents, Jean V. Naggar and Jennifer Weltz, loved the book, kept the faith and guided me with gentle realism and professionalism through the first edition.

A special thanks to Adriene Marshall and Janet Patterson Verdeguer for perceptive editing and for helping me market the revised book. *(And also for letting me get away with some incorrect grammar here and there because I thought it expressed what I wanted to say in a more conversational way.)*

I feel that, in writing this book, I stand on the shoulders of many giants in the fields of psychology and self-help. I have tried to make their ideas simple and accessible, and to credit their wonderful ideas each place I have mentioned them. The really special ones become so familiar over time that they seem like part of my own practice and coaching. So if I have inadvertently omitted credit to anyone, I apologize. The responsibility is completely my own.

Resources and References

Books and Articles:

* = Highly Recommended

American Psychological Association (See Mazure, Carolyn M., *Understanding Depression in Women)*

Bader, Ellyn and Peter T. Pearson. *In Quest of the Mythical Mate: A Developmental Approach to Diagnosis and Treatment in Couples Therapy.* Brunner/Mazel, Taylor-Francis Group, 1988.

Campbell, Chellie. *The Wealthy Spirit.* Sourcebooks, Inc., 2002.

*Davis, Michele Weiner. *Change Your Life and Everyone In It.* Simon & Schuster Adult Publishing Group, First Fireside Edition, 1996.

Doherty, William J. *Take Back Your Marriage: Sticking Together in a World That Pulls Us Apart.* Guilford Publications, 2001.

Ferber, Richard M.D. *Solve Your Child's Sleep Problem.* Fireside, 1986.

*Glass, Shirley P. with Jean Coppock Staeheli. *Not "Just Friends": Protect Your Relationship from Infidelity and Heal the Trauma of Betrayal.* The Free Press, 2003.

Gottman, John M. and Nan Silver. *The Seven Principles to Making Marriage Work: A Practical Guide from the*

Country's Foremost Relationship Expert. Three Rivers Press, 2000.

Granju, Katie Allison, Betsy Kennedy and William Sears. *Attachment Parenting: Instinctive Care for Your Baby and Young Child.* Pocket Books, 1999.

Hahn, Thich Nhat and Anh Huong Nguyen. *Walking Meditation* w/DVD and CD-ROM.

Illsey Clarke, Jean, Ph.D., Connie Dawson, Ph.D., and David Bredehoft, Ph.D. *How Much Is Enough: Everything You Need to Know to Steer Clear of Overindulgence and Raise Likeable, Responsible and Respectful Children.* Da Capo Press, 2004.

Johnson, Susan M. *Emotionally Focused Couple Therapy with Trauma Survivors: Strengthening Attachment Bonds.* The Guilford Press, 2005.

*Johnson, Dr. Sue. *Hold Me Tight: Seven Conversations for a Lifetime of Love.* Little, Brown and Company, 2008. Also in Audio.

Kabat-Zinn, Jon, Ph.D. *Full Catastrophe Living.* Bantum-Dell, 2005. Also in Audio.

Lerner, Harriet, Ph.D. *The Mother Dance: How Children Change Your Life.* HarperCollins, 1998.

Mazure, Carolyn M., Ph.D. and Gwendolyn Puryear Keita, Ph.D. *Understanding Depression in Women: Applying Empirical Research to Practice and Policy.* APA Books, 2006.

*Pantley, Elizabeth. *The No-Cry Sleep Solution: Gentle Ways to Help Your Baby Sleep Through the Night.* McGraw-Hill Companies, 2002.

Pittman, Frank. *Private Lies: Infidelity and the Betrayal of Intimacy.* W. W. Norton & Co., 1990.

Rubin, Gretchen. *The Happiness Project.* HarperCollins Publishers, 2009.

Shimoff, Marci with Carol Kline. *Happy for No Reason.* Free Press, 2008.

Shapiro, Francine. *Eye Movement Desensitization and Reprocessing: Basic Principles, Protocols and Procedures,* 2nd edition. The Guilford Press, New York, 2001.

Thevenin, Tine. *The Family Bed.* 1987.

Tipping, Colin. *Radical Forgiveness.* Sounds True, Inc., 2009.

Walls, Jeanette. *The Glass Castle.* Simon & Shuster, 2005.

* Highly Recommended

Performance

Becker, Rob. *Defending the Caveman.* Broadway comedy, debuted in San Francisco, 1991.

Video

How the Grinch Stole Christmas. Director Ron Howard, 2000.

Prancer. Director John D. Hancock, 1989.

Websites

www.cavemania.com

www.comamas.com

www.cullagunabeach.com

www.iceeft.com

www.insightmeditioncenter.org

www.fathersforum.com

www.doctorcarol.com

www.parentsplace.com

www.smartmarriages.com

Credits and Permissions

Front cover

Cartoon Strips

About Dr. Carol

If you enjoyed this book, you might want to contact Dr. Carol for individual or couple coaching sessions to guide you through some of the problems you may be experiencing. Dr. Carol is available for office visits in Laguna Beach, Calif. Some clients prefer email or phone consultations. For more information, visit her professional website www.cullagunabeach.com where there are details about her extensive background and experience, her specialties, and how the sessions work. Call her office for more information or to set an appointment: (949) 494-5432.

Couple Vision Weekend Retreat

Spend a weekend with your spouse in beautiful Laguna Beach! You'll enjoy lovely surroundings, great food, hiking, sports, activities, rest, relaxation … at the same time create a Couple Vision that will change your lives forever. You'll have three private sessions with Dr. Carol over the weekend as you "Become one of those couples that some people envy," by improving both your relationship and your marriage. Email carol@doctorcarol.com or call her office: (949) 494-5432.

Intro to Couple Vision Webinars

Dr. Carol frequently schedules free "Intro to Couple Vision" webinars. In these one-hour sessions, you will learn a process for creating your overall lifestyle plan: how you want your lives to be and how you are going to work together to make your vision come true. Attendees receive a free PDF download of Dr. Carol's Couple Vision Planner. Go to www.doctorcarol.com for dates, times and registration link. Continue through the process on your own, or schedule personal counseling with Dr. Carol. These sessions can take place in her office, or via phone or email: (949) 494-5432.

What They're Saying About Couple Vision

"I create Mission-Vision Statements all the time for my job. I never considered creating one for my marriage!" – *E.G.*

"Our Couple Vision helped us improve our finances, our sex life, our parenting, and gave our relationship more meaning." – *Marilyn H.*

"Our Vision process taught us that when we disagree, it leads to creative solutions." – *Phyllis P.*

"Couple Vision helped us get our hearts (and heads) together right before retirement." – *Fred and Gwen*

Corporations, Organizations, Non-Profits

Happily Married With Kids: It's Not a Fairy Tale is available at quantity discounts with bulk purchase for educational, business, sales promotion or philanthropic purposes. Special cover printing is available. For information, please telephone Special Markets Department, Granny Apple Publishing, LLC at (941) 870-3422.

Made in the USA
San Bernardino, CA
23 September 2013